PRAISE FOR SUSAN OMILIAN'S WORK IN THE THRIVER ZONE

"This book offers faith, courage and dignity to women who have survived the destructive and selfish actions of abusive men. Susan's message is 'Don't settle for anything less than a life that is better than ever.' She knows that women can do it and by the time a woman has worked her way through this excellent guidebook for healing, she will believe it, too."

— LUNDY BANCROFT, AUTHOR, *WHY DOES HE DO THAT?: INSIDE THE MINDS OF ANGRY AND CONTROLLING MEN* AND *DAILY WISDOM FOR WHY DOES HE DO THAT?*

"Susan's book will touch a responsive chord in women who have been abused and those who advocate for them. Susan's creativity, her inspirational workshops and her own personal journey make this book a 'must read' for anyone interested in the empowerment of women."

— ALYCE LaVIOLETTE, MS, MFT, AUTHOR, *IT COULD HAPPEN TO ANYONE: WHY BATTERED WOMEN STAY*

"Susan begins with a rare insight – that what makes a battered woman is not what the abuser has done to her but what he has kept her from doing for herself – and then takes her readers on a jubilant journey of self-realization. On the way, Susan helps them remake their world and get back in touch with their power and possibility."

— EVAN STARK PhD, MSW, PROFESSOR, SCHOOL OF PUBLIC AFFAIRS AND ADMINISTRATION, RUTGERS UNIVERSITY-NEWARK AND AUTHOR OF *COERCIVE CONTROL: HOW MEN ENTRAP WOMEN IN PERSONAL LIFE*

"As a social worker and therapist who works with women with depression and trauma histories that frequently include domestic violence, I have found Susan's work to be an invaluable resource. I especially like the exercises Susan has developed that bolsters the hopes and dreams of my clients and help them realize that they can succeed if they know what they value and care about. This book gives them great hope for the future and connects them with Susan and her story in a very personal way."

— KATHY G. NOVAK, MSW, LCSW

"Susan is a talented, gifted and committed healer with a heartfelt message that enables those who have suffered to dare to hope again. Her book is not only timely, but timeless as well."

— ANITA SWANSON, RN, AUTHOR, *SLOW HOPE, THE LONG JOURNEY HOME*

"Susan has transformed the lives of countless survivors of abuse with her compassionate, effective work."

— KATHRYN TULL , MA, LMFT, AUTHOR, *NEXT BOLD STEP: LEARNING TO LOVE AND VALUE YOURSELF, AND KNOW THAT YOU MATTER!*

"Susan is incredibly driven and motivated to make a positive change in the lives of women. Inspired and fueled by the murder of her niece, Susan has taken an experience which for many leads to anger, resentment, and frustration and has instead converted that energy into creating something for the greater good. She believes every woman, especially those who have been victimized, deserve the chance for a new start and to live a life which is filled with success, abundance, and happiness."

— HEATHER FREEMAN, FOUNDER OF THE GUTSY GIRL CLUB

"I will definitely put the exercises in Susan's book to work with my clients and support groups, and refer them to your amazing workshops. Susan's training about her work and materials was one of the best I have ever attended!"

— CAMPUS ADVOCATE, SEXUAL ASSAULT CRISIS COUNSELOR

"With Susan's help, I have transcended and transformed from merely surviving this life into the higher realms of THRIVING! I have retrieved parts of my soul that have been missing for a long time. These pieces of my soul are so happy to be reunited with the rest of me that they want to come out and play and share the joy of being whole and complete."

— ADRIENNE, A WORKSHOP PARTICIPANT

"Susan has a magic and that magic is highly contagious to those who spend even a little bit of time in her presence. That magic comes from removing the tragedy and abuse out of our future life equation. Susan gives us her support, never-ending encouragement, and her true self. Every exercise supports this experience, one is not better than the next, they build upon each other. We allow ourselves to thrive and this powerful gift ends the bondage of surviving."

— LORA, A WORKSHOP PARTICIPANT

"The material Susan has developed allowed me to address the fears and self-doubt that I had carried around with me for 30 plus years. The writing exercises helped me to articulate and own my feelings and learn techniques to quiet my Inner Critic. Both of these exercises enabled me to move forward with my life in a safe and supportive environment that Susan provide. Now I am thriving along with a whole community of women who Susan has helped!"

— TRISH, A CAREER COACH AND JOB SEARCH PROFESSIONAL

Entering the Thriver Zone

A Seven-Step Guide to Thriving After Abuse

Susan M. Omilian, JD

Reclaiming the Lives of Women
Who Have Been Abused

BUTTERFLY BLISS PRODUCTIONS LLC
West Hartford, CT

Entering the Thriver Zone: A Seven-Step Guide to Thriving After Abuse

Butterfly Bliss Productions LLC
P.O. Box 330482, West Hartford, CT 06133
ButterflyBlissProductions.com
ThriverZone.com
SusanOmilian.com

ISBN # 978-0-9842509-2-9 printed book
ISBN # 978-0-9842509-3-6 e-book

Worksheets referenced in the text can be downloaded at "Resources" on *ThriverZone.com*.

Author photo by Cynthia Lang Photography
Maggie's photo by Joe Sherman | *PhotographicArtistry.net*
Front cover & interior design by Donna Gentile Creative | *DonnaGentileCreative.com*
Back cover & spine design by Another Jones Graphics | *AnotherJones.com*

A portion of the proceeds of this book will be donated to services for women and children who have experienced abuse and violence.

Library of Congress Cataloging-in-Publication Data
Names: Omilian, Susan M.
Title: Entering the Thriver Zone : a seven-step guide to thriving after abuse/ Susan M. Omilian JD.
Description: West Hartford, CT : Butterfly Bliss Productions LLC, [2016] | Series: [The Thriver Zone series] ; [book 1] | "Reclaiming the lives of women who have been abused." | Includes bibliographical references.
Identifiers: ISBN 978-0-9842509-2-9 (print) | ISBN 978-0-9842509-3-6 (ebook)
Subjects: LCSH: Abused women--Psychology. | Happiness. | Self-realization in women. | Goal (Psychology)
Classification: LCC HV6626 .O45 2016 (print) | HV6626 (ebook) | DDC 362.8292--dc23

Printed in the United States of America

DEDICATION

Dedicated to my niece Maggie (1980 – 1999)

As Maggie's amazing life and tragic death have inspired me,
I hope that this book will inspire other women
to become the person they have always wanted to be.

Maggie would have been outraged by the way she died.
I call upon her every day to help me put down my mantle of grief,
dream my wildest dreams and not let my fears hold me back.

For me, this is Maggie's legacy!

~ Susan M. Omilian ~

Living well is the best revenge!
— GEORGE HERBERT

ACKNOWLEDGMENTS

For all the women, survivors of abuse, who have worked with me over the last fifteen or more years, I admire your courage, persistence and refusal to let what has happened to you define who you are. A special thank you to those who agreed to appear in this book, particularly those who shared their thriver success stories — Susy, Donna, Betsy, Sophia and Vanessa as well as Pat, Dot, Cecile, Brenda, Samantha and Cynthia.

I want to thank my brother Rick and sister-in-law Martha, who as Maggie's stepfather and mother, have been fellow travelers with me on this amazing journey. I also want to thank my brother Frank and sister-in-law Cathie, my sister Elaine and brother-in-law Wally, and my niece Lindsey and her husband Matt, for all their support. I wish Mom and Dad could be here to share this moment, but I have my extended family — my wonderful aunts, uncles and cousins — who are all very special to me. Thanks for supporting me with your love as well as your great generosity of heart.

Thanks to Donna Gentile, amazing book designer and graphic artist, Claudia Volkman for her keen eye in proofreading this book and Sharon Castlen for her support, guidance and remarkable vision in marketing this book.

Most of all, thanks to all who have let me share your journey as you have shared mine to discovering the life we were destined to live and the work that we were born to do.

There is no greater gift!

ABOUT THE AUTHOR

An attorney, author and motivational speaker, Susan Omilian has worked extensively as an advocate to end violence against women for the past forty years. In the 1970s, she founded

a rape crisis center and represented battered women in divorce proceedings in the early 1980s. She also litigated sex discrimination cases including helping to articulate the legal concept that made sexual harassment illegal in the 1990s.

She is a published author of several books on sex discrimination law as well as articles for newspapers and journals including *The Voice: The Journal of the Battered Women's Movement* published by the National Coalition Against Domestic Violence (NCADV). Susan holds a law degree from Wayne State University in Detroit and a bachelor of arts degree in journalism from the University of Michigan. She is licensed to practice law in both Connecticut and Michigan.

With the death of her nineteen-year-old niece Maggie who was shot and killed in October, 1999 by her ex-boyfriend, Susan's work on behalf of women became more personal and immediate. She vowed to help other women move on after abuse and create a new life for themselves and their children as Maggie could not.

SUSAN'S PERSONAL MISSION STATEMENT

"I am a woman of power whose mission in life is to be a catalyst for change for victims of violence against women. Today I celebrate my life by building a community of strong, independent, productive women who have survived abuse and are thriving in well-being, love and joy."

ABOUT THE SPEAKER

Susan Omilian is an experienced, inspirational speaker with a dramatic story and a unique motivational model to share. She has helped hundreds of women reclaim their lives after abuse and take the journey from victim to survivor to "thriver!"

As the award-winning originator and facilitator since 2001 of My Avenging Angel Workshops™ based on the idea that "living well is the best revenge," Susan has developed a seven-step process to thriving after abuse. It has been described as "life-changing" and as "a component for women recovering from abuse that has been virtually overlooked." Susan delivers her message of hope and possibility for women with passion and enthusiasm fueled by her own personal tragedy — her niece Maggie's violent death. It is her firm belief that women who take the journey to thriving are less likely to return to an abusive relationship or suffer the long-term physical and psychological consequences of the abuse they have experienced.

Susan is a recognized, articulate national expert on the process of recovery after violence and abuse. She has been invited to speak throughout the country by victim rights organizations such as National Organization of Victim Assistance (NOVA), before service providers and clinicians as well as to students and faculty on college campuses. She has also been a keynote speaker at domestic violence and sexual assault awareness events as well as a featured presenter at national meetings and international conferences sponsored by the Institute on Violence, Abuse and Trauma (IVAT).

With simple, invigorating writing exercises and inspirational success stories, Susan's book, *Entering the Thriver Zone: A Seven-Step Guide to Thriving After Abuse* sets forth the motivational guidance she has successfully used with women over the last fifteen years. Susan envisions that millions of women who have faced violence and abuse as well as their families, friends, counselors, therapists and health care providers, will find her book an invaluable guide to taking the life-changing journey from victim to survivor to thriver!

For more information about Susan's transformational work or to arrange for her to speak, please visit *ThriverZone.com*.

CONTENTS

Grieve not

nor speak of me with tears, but laugh

and talk of me

as though I were beside you.

I loved you so.

`Twas Heaven here with you.

– ISLA PASCHAL RICHARDSON
AND THE EPITAPH ON MAGGIE'S GRAVE

NOTE FROM THE AUTHOR —
MAGGIE'S STORY AND A NEW BEGINNING

In the early morning hours of October 18, 1999, I got a phone call from my sister.

"It's Maggie," she said, her voice trembling. "She's been shot. She's dead."

I couldn't believe it. Maggie, my brother's nineteen-year-old stepdaughter, had been murdered at school by her ex-boyfriend who then killed himself. It was another senseless act of violence but this time, Maggie — our Maggie — was dead.

For years, I had worked as an attorney advocating for women's rights, but Maggie's death made working to end violence against women more personal and immediate for me. If this could happen to my family and to Maggie, it could happen to anyone. But what was I being called to do?

One morning it came to me. I was thinking about the power of the moment when a woman decides to leave the abuse. I realized that Maggie did not live beyond her moment, but suddenly I imagined myself working with other women who could transform their lives after abuse. After all, wasn't getting on with one's life the most exacting revenge against a man who had tried to bend that woman to his will?

By then I could see that for those of us who face a "life-altering event" such as abuse, the death of a loved one, divorce or the loss of a job, there is either a road to recovery that brings new vigor and purpose to our lives or a spiraling down into anger, depression and hopelessness.

I realized that I had stumbled onto a more productive path, one where I could:

- discover opportunity in what felt like loss
- focus on positive emotions to move me forward
- celebrate the life I had, living in the present, not past, and
- dare to create the life I so richly deserved

How could I work with women who had been abused so that they too could be similarly transformed? Slowly I envisioned a workshop, inspired by the quote, *"Living well is the best revenge."* Sure I wanted to avenge Maggie's death, but with a lighter touch like an angel's and without anger or recrimination. So I coined the name "My Avenging Angel," and I saw the workshops as the critical "next step" for women to help them move beyond abuse and restore the positive energy in their lives. Now with this book, I want to send out the unique materials I have developed in the workshops to more women across this country and around the world. I want them to realize the amazing possibility of thriving after abuse.

Is this work easy? Hardly. I have heard so many stories from women of abuse, betrayal and dashed hopes that I wish I had a magic wand to simply wave away their pain and anguish. They have suffered greatly. At times, their self-esteem is low and they have little belief that their lives will ever get better. But they do have hope. Each time I give them the choice of reliving the abuse and the pain inflicted on them or reaching deep down inside to uncover their true heart's desires, they do choose the latter. They set goals for themselves that are not only achievable, but also can spur them on to making bigger and better changes for themselves.

I can now see that the process of reconnecting to positive energy in one's life is the movement from victim to survivor to thriver. I have traveled this journey myself since Maggie's death and have taught it in a seven-step process to hundreds of women in the My Avenging Angel Workshops™. I have encouraged and challenged them to see that with this more positive perspective as a thriver, they can too regain their power and reclaim their lives.

But having a positive outlook on life is hard for survivors of abuse and loss. It really gets to us sometimes that everyone else seems to have an easier life, a more comfortable journey or a less challenging existence. But now I know that the truest measure of our lives is not what we have experienced, but what we have made of our experiences.

We don't really know how good it can get once we get positive and focus our energies on our future, not the past. Whatever we might have imagined for ourselves is only a fraction of what we can have when we free ourselves to live well, be happy and create the life we want. Then living well is not only the best revenge; it is, in fact, the song of our soul and the fulfillment of all our dreams.

— Susan Omilian

HOW TO USE THIS BOOK

YES, YOU ARE A WRITER!

You can do the writing exercises in this book that guide you through the Seven Steps to Thriving After Abuse. If you are afraid someone might see what you have written, write on a piece of paper and then destroy it. You don't have to keep what you write. Just get it out there for a while and let it shine!

WORKING FROM WRITING PROMPTS IS EASY!

When you see ✍ throughout this book, it means it's time to write from a "writing prompt!" A writing prompt is simply a way into your writing. Let it take you where it will, even if what you write has nothing to do with the prompt. Keep writing. Don't stop! Don't worry about spelling, grammar or if what you wrote doesn't make any sense! If you like printable copies of the worksheets in this book, go to *thriverzone.com* and click on WORKSHEETS.

DECORATE YOUR OWN JOURNAL.

Before you start writing, buy yourself a composition book or notebook and decorate the cover! Use pictures from magazines or photos from your own life as well as stickers or glitter glue to bling it up! You deserve it!

INVITE A FRIEND TO JOIN YOU! FORM YOUR OWN THRIVER GROUP!

Get together with a group of your friends and THRIVE! Visit ThriverZone.com to learn how. Find more writing prompts and exercises there. You can work through this book by yourself or invite a friend or group of friends to do it with you. Writing, reading and sharing the experience with other women is a fabulous thing to do.

THERE ARE NO RULES!

You can't do this wrong! Don't worry—you can do it! Visit thriverzone.com to learn how. Find more writing prompts and exercises there.

Getting Started

SEVEN STEPS TO THRIVING AFTER ABUSE

No longer a victim, beyond a survivor, she is a thriver on the brink of a new life.
She's a new breed of woman moving on after abuse, and she wants her revenge.
Living well is her best revenge. She is pushing through her fears, finding
positive energy and forging a new future for herself and her children.

Are you ready? Are you strong, courageous and bold enough to take this amazing journey to reclaim your life? Can you see yourself moving from victim to survivor to thriver and permanently breaking the cycle of violence and trauma in your life?

If you want to launch yourself into a new world of limitless possibilities, you are not alone. In the past, women subjected to trauma, violence and abuse had little recourse to leave an abusive relationship or move through the crisis of a sexual assault. Today so many more of us can stand on the edge of a new life that we barely dared to imagine and savor an abuse-free environment, cheering "I'm free!" But what about the next question: "Now what?"

I have an answer to that for you. If you are highly motivated to transform your life but don't know how, I have developed a motivational model using writing exercises and interactive activities to take you on a journey beyond abuse. It is a journey of spirit into the right-brain world of your imagination. There, unlimited creative possibilities lie, your wounded spirit can be revived and the dreams that you have long set aside for a better, more satisfying life can finally come true.

The idea of this journey to wholeness is the most innovative aspect of the work I have done for the last fifteen years with women who have been abused. Using a seven-step process that promotes growth and renewed self-confidence, I have seen women transform their lives and do amazing things. That same amazing transformation now awaits you! Take the journey to not just survive, but thrive after abuse.

CHOOSING YOUR PATH

I see two paths that women who may have experienced abuse can take on the journey to becoming a "thriver."

#1 — FOR WOMEN WHO HAVE YET TO IDENTIFY THEMSELVES AS VICTIMS OF ABUSE

Before my nineteen-year-old niece was murdered by her ex-boyfriend, Maggie never saw herself as a victim of abuse. He had never physically assaulted her, and she missed all the other warning signs that she was in a potentially dangerous relationship. Take a look at the list on the next page, The Warning Signs of an Unhealthy, Abusive Relationship. A list similar to this one was handed out on the college campus a week after Maggie was killed there. When Maggie's friends saw it, they were shocked to realize that her ex-boyfriend had done everything on that list, including isolating her from her family and friends, except that he had never hit her or threatened her physically. No one saw how much danger she was in, not even Maggie. She didn't realize that his abusive behavior could escalate to violence when she dared to leave him and he refused to accept the termination of their relationship and let her go. (For more about Maggie's story, see Note from the Author.)

Since Maggie's moment of realizing she was a victim of abuse was the moment of her death, she did not survive to move on to the healing part of her journey. Like Maggie, you may be a woman who has not yet thought of herself as an abused woman or a victim of violence. But if you recognize yourself somewhere on the pages of this book, it is my hope and desire that you will take action to leave an abusive relationship as soon as you safely can or deal with a sexual assault as you may not have in the past.

If you haven't identified yourself as a victim before reading this book, you may need to spend more time in the "victim" stage of your journey, getting yourself safe and expressing a whole range of feelings with a counselor or therapist about how being a victim has been impacted your life.

For immediate crisis intervention services in your local community, call the **National Domestic Violence Hotline 800-799-SAFE (7233)** or **800-787-3224 (TTY for the deaf)** and visit *www.ndvh.org* or the **National Sexual Assault Hotline 800-656-HOPE (4673)**, operated by the **Rape, Abuse & Incest National Network (RAINN)** and *visit www.rainn.org.*

WARNING SIGNS OF AN UNHEALTHY, ABUSIVE RELATIONSHIP

He is controlling, possessive and overly demanding of her time and attention. He appears at times to be two different people: one, charming, loving and kind; the other, abusive, vicious and mean—like "Dr. Jekyll and Mr. Hyde." He keeps her on edge, not knowing who he'll be. He makes her feel bad about herself and will, at times, be sorry for his behavior, promising not to do it again. But he will do it again and then deny, minimize or blame others for his behavior. She will feel it is all her fault. If only she could please him more or be more compliant, he wouldn't treat her this way.

EMOTIONAL
- He insults her, calls her names and belittles her in private and in public with her family and friends.
- He isolates her from family and friends, forbidding her to see them or limiting her access to them.
- He is jealous of her contact with others, particularly with other men. He exaggerates her relationships with other men, accusing her unfairly of having affairs outside of their relationship.
- He wants to know where she is at all times, calling or texting her to find out who she is with. He invades her privacy by checking her cell phone, viewing her email or monitoring her web pages.
- He refuses to accept when she ends the relationship and may stalk her long afterwards.

PHYSICAL
- He yells, screams and loses his temper easily, sometimes disproportionately over unimportant things.
- He destroys her things, kicks or breaks other property, making her fear that he could hurt her, too.
- He intimidates her, making her afraid of him by his looks, actions and gestures.
- He grabs her, kicks her, slaps her, punches her, strangles her or draws a gun or weapon and threatens to kill her. He harms her pets or threatens to hurt or harm her family or friends.
- He stalks her with unwanted phone calls, visits to her house or job and secretly monitors her actions.

ECONOMIC
- He controls her access to money, even her own money or money she has earned herself.
- He refuses to pay bills or let her know about family income, investments or property.
- He keeps her from getting or keeping a job, refuses to support their family or children.
- He makes all the big decisions, using male privilege to get his way and insisting on rigid gender roles.

PSYCHOLOGICAL
- She feels like she is going crazy, that his view of the world is not reasonable, but she will have little chance of convincing him otherwise and he demands her absolute loyalty to his way of thinking.
- He says he can't live without her or will kill himself if she leaves, so she fears ending the relationship.
- He pushes the relationship too far, too fast and is obsessed with her and wants her for himself.
- He has unrealistic expectations and demands, and she feels it is her fault he's not happy.

SEXUAL
- He demands to have sex forcibly without her consent with him or with others.
- He withdraws sex from her or makes it conditional on her compliance to his demands.
- He calls her crude names, implying she is promiscuous and unfaithful sexually to him.

For more information on the Duluth Power and Control Wheel, see *theduluthmodel.org*.

SIGNS OF A HEALTHY RELATIONSHIP

In a healthy relationship, the two people are on an equal footing and they respect, trust and support each other. They are honest with each other and take responsibility for their actions. They are good parents, sharing responsibility in raising their kids. They have an economic partnership in which the best interests of both are considered, and they communicate, negotiate and treat each other fairly.

Consult the Resources section of this book for information on how to contact needed services and support. In addition, you may want to explore the books and websites in the Resources section of this book regarding Post-Traumatic Stress Disorder (PTSD), an anxiety disorder that some people may experience after being subjected to abuse and trauma. It is reported that 84 percent of women who are abused suffer PTSD, and between 22 to 35 percent of the women who visit emergency departments in the United States are there for symptoms related to ongoing abuse. More than one-half of women who are sexually assaulted may develop PTSD, also known as "rape trauma syndrome." Not everyone who is abused or assaulted will experience PTSD, but its symptoms are easily recognizable, and there are counselors who can help you deal with its effects on your life.

#2 — FOR WOMEN SURVIVORS OF DOMESTIC VIOLENCE, SEXUAL ASSAULT OR OTHER ABUSE

You are among the nearly one quarter of the women in the United States, more than 12 million, who will be abused by a current or former partner sometime during your lifetime. Hopefully, this book can help you find a journey beyond what you may have endured in your lifetime as a victim and a survivor of abuse and violence.

When I first worked on violence against women issues many years ago, there were few services to help women identify themselves as victims so that they can survive domestic violence or sexual assault. Most people today don't realize that it wasn't until the late 1960s and early 1970s that sexual assault crisis centers were established, and domestic violence programs did not appear until the 1980s. Before that, these crimes against women had no names and few services were available to victims. Today, a whole new generation of women and children will survive domestic violence and sexual assault because of a strong network of crisis intervention services in many communities across this country. Women will identify themselves as victims and receive support to become survivors of abuse. But I believe there is another step for all of us beyond merely surviving, and that is becoming a thriver in spite of what we have experienced.

VICTIM ➪ SURVIVOR ➪ THRIVER

This is the critical next step beyond surviving abuse to that of becoming a "thriver."

What is a thriver? Here's a working definition I have developed and we'll be using throughout this book.

A thriver is a happy, self-confident and productive individual who believes she has a prosperous life ahead of her. She is primed to follow her dreams, go back to school, find a new job, start her own business or write her story. She believes in herself and in her future so much that she will not return to an abusive relationship. She speaks knowledgeably and confidently about her experiences and is not stuck in her anger or need for revenge.

Living well is her best revenge!

Helping women to reach this critical "next step" on the journey beyond abuse is the goal of my work. Lora, a woman who attended one of my workshops several years ago, described her journey to surviving and beyond this way:

I had done a lot work before I met Susan, attempting to make the best of a bad situation, dressing up my existence and trying to make life choices that wouldn't victimize me. I knew I was no longer a victim. I had learned how to manage not to be that, but I was always wearing my 'survivor' armor. The armor was heavy and it defined who I was and my limiting circumstances.

What a wonderful description of the "armor" or shell that we as survivors wear as a result of what we have endured. We are heavily burdened with low self-esteem, emotional fear, shame, guilt and hopelessness, the inevitable impacts of being abused and violated in our society today. Many of us are depressed, appear lost or are suffering from physical problems, and most are deeply afraid that their lives will never get any better. In this state of mind, we believe, like Lora, that the impacts of abuse and violence will forever define our lives as limited and permanently damaged. Sometimes, this damage is evident by the looks of pain on our faces or in the way we carry our bodies or talk about the future. We live with the hope that someone, somewhere can make it all better. We'll even accept a "band-aid" approach, just so the pain, fear and disappointment will stop for some period of time.

Lora describes her state of mind coming into this work:

When I went to the first session of Susan's workshop, I didn't know what to expect. My expectations were of an open forum where each of us would tell our stories and grieve our sorry existences together with Susan's support. Luckily, that was not Susan's intention. Susan was simply asking me to remove my armor and consider a part of me untouched by the abuse. Could this part of me put the abuse aside and motivate me to search for my true passion? I knew this part of myself, not well, but I believed there was a center core that no one had disturbed. Susan encouraged me to invite that part out and talk awhile, dream awhile and grieve our years of separation. Listening to the experiences of others, as well, was key to opening this part of me.

I call opening up to that part of us that is untouched by the abuse, finding or making contact with the Thriver or the Happy Person Inside You.

MOVING BEYOND SURVIVOR TO A "LIFE-ALTERING" MOMENT

What might motivate you to take the journey to thriving? Are you really satisfied with merely surviving? Are you, like Lora, really good at surviving? Or are you willing to take the journey and find that "life-altering" moment?

Mine came with my niece Maggie's death, and it set me on my path to finding the work that I was destined to do in this lifetime. It finally answered the question I had been asking all my life: "Why am I here on this earth?" In fact, right after Maggie's death, it became very clear to me that everything I had ever done in my life had come to the moment of her death. Every skill I had learned, every experience I had had, every person I had ever met — it was all in preparation for her death and what I would be propelled to do as a result of it.

Suddenly, everything made sense. It was a "life-altering" moment!

I figured that if something this tragic didn't get me to my purpose in life, nothing else ever would. Most importantly, I came to see that my journey wasn't outside of me — something that

I had always been waiting for, such as a better job, more money or a meaningful relationship. It was a journey inside me, to find the person I was always meant to be. Ultimately, this terrible tragedy filled me with so much positive energy that it finally taught me to live in the present, not the past, and believe in myself completely. Finally, I found that this new, magnificent me saved me. But I didn't make this transformation simply to save myself. I wanted something really big to happen so that Maggie would not have died in vain. The "big thing" that did happen was that I was now in a position to help others, and I had been wanting to find myself in that kind of moment for a very long, long time.

The only question was if I would have the courage to go for it and let myself shine out to the whole world!

To find the inner wisdom and resources to begin this journey, I had to first realize that this is work I will never get done in this lifetime. In fact, I hope I never get it done. Every day, I happily embrace the new challenges in my life and work to find the courage not to be afraid as I take them on. Before Maggie's death, questions like "Why do bad things always happen to me?" haunted me. Now each day, I ask myself instead, "What have you accomplished today that is meaningful and helpful to another human being?"

Discovering the thriver spirit inside me was a surprise. I had never seen myself as spiritual before Maggie's death. But with her death, I was able to strip away that which is false and limiting about me. I touched the essence of what I am and who I am meant to be in this lifetime, and that discovery has given me great joy. As crazy as it may sound, with Maggie's death I was given a gift. It was a wake-up call for me to stop focusing on what was missing in my life and find something good to hold onto. What I realized in this transformation is that I am on a spiritual journey. It is leading me to do meaningful work and find a community of like-minded individuals who have a similar life purpose.

Today, my personal Mission Statement reflects that feeling. It reads:

I am a woman of power whose mission in life is to be a catalyst for change for victims of violence against women. Today I celebrate my life by building a community of strong, independent, productive women who have survived abuse and are thriving in well-being, love and joy.

This is my life, who I truly am, and, for the first time, I am happy. I am thriving! I am living the life I had always imagined I would.

It is a true gift indeed that has come from a loss of great, tragic proportions!

WHERE ARE YOU ON YOUR JOURNEY?

So where are you on your life's journey? What do you need to do in order to make a similar transformation and find the thriver inside you? Where are you stuck?

If you have found this book, you are probably close to transformation, but you may need some help to create a new, wonderful life for yourself and your children. Lora did it, and here's how she describes her transformation.

I am bigger than my former story. The center core [the thriver] that Susan helped me to discover knows this to be true. It motivates me to forgive myself, forgive those who have abused me and excuse myself from the 'survivor' life course for something more rewarding, more authentic and definitely more satisfying.

HOW DO YOU RATE?

Let's say that you are in transformation now, even if it doesn't feel like you are. The first thing we need to determine is what is holding you back from moving forward to the place you were born to discover and live in for the rest of your life. It's time to survey the thoughts and beliefs you have that are influencing your life right now as well as your future plans.

It is always good at times to review not only what you are thinking and feeling, but also your hopes and dreams. The survey on the next page is designed to do so. Take a quick moment to review it and then write your answers in your journal or notebook. Yes, do it quickly! Don't think about your answers too much. Let them come from your heart, not your head.

Go for it now! Let's see what you can learn about yourself today, and then we'll review what it means for your future!

SURVEY FOR JOURNEY TO THRIVING

Always feel this way	Sometimes feel this way	Never feel this way	
			I'm too busy for quiet time to think about where I'm going.
			There is no way I can create the life I want right now.
			There are some voices inside my head that are very critical of me, and I'll never get them to quiet down.
			Sometimes I feel there's a happy person inside of me who wants to get out.
			My biggest fear is that I'll never get my life together.
			Bad things always seem to happen to me.
			I'll never figure out who I am or what I want to be when I grow up.
			I don't take any big risks. Life is too scary.
			Abuse has always been in my life. I can't do much about it.
			It's hard to find other people who have gone through what I have and want to change their lives.
			Taking time for me is a selfish thing to do.

If I could change one thing about my life, I'd ...

_____

If I had $10 million and all the time to do whatever I wanted, I'd ...

_____

_____

REVIEW YOUR RESULTS

Let's look at what you came up with on the survey. Was any particular statement difficult for you to answer? Which statements were easiest to answer?

In what areas did you mark that you "always feel this way?" Any surprises?

Write about that now in your journal or notebook.

Look at your "sometimes" responses. Are they in areas that you feel you might be able to move into the "always" category? What would be your barriers to doing so?

Write about that now in your journal or notebook.

Now let's review your answer to "If I had $10 million and all the time to do whatever I wanted to do, I'd…" Did anything surprise you there? How possible is that dream for you? What are your obstacles, besides time and money?

Write about that now in your journal or notebook.

LOOK AT YOUR BELIEFS ABOUT YOURSELF

Have you noticed that the statements on this survey are all limiting beliefs about yourself and the impact of abuse on your life? What the survey actually measures is your self-esteem, how you feel about yourself as a person. Our self-esteem rises and falls with the experiences we face in life. This survey can help you identify the areas that you might want to work on. For example:

If you checked any of these in the "always" or "sometimes" box —

I'm too busy for quiet time to think about where I'm going.
Taking time for me is a selfish thing to do.
It's hard to find other people who've gone through what I have and want to change their lives.

— you may have some limiting beliefs about taking time for yourself and finding others to support you on your journey. Try some affirmations like "I'm worth it!" and "Taking care of myself is not selfish!" See more on affirmations at the end of this chapter and in Step 2, Quiet the Inner Critic.

Let's look at another group on the list —

> *There is no way I can create the life I want right now.*
> *My biggest fear is that I'll never get my life together.*
> *I'll never figure out who I am or what I want to be when I grow up.*
> *I don't take any big risks. Life is too scary.*

If you put any of these in the "always" or "sometimes" category, I'd say that you have hit on the limiting beliefs that are hardest for you to move from. But as you go through this book, you'll find exercises to help you build positive energy, quiet your fears and discover a rich, rewarding future. Look at Step 4, Get Positive Energy; Step 6, Overcome Fears, and Step 7, Set New Goals.

If the survey indicated that you "always" or "sometimes" feel that —

> *Abuse has always been in my life. There's not much I can do about it.*
> *Bad things always seem to happen to me.*

— think about how your experiences have limited you in the past and how you now want to find opportunity in those experiences to grow and change.

Can you find opportunity in loss? Yes, I believe you can and you'll find out how to do so later in this book.

If you've marked "always" or "sometimes" for —

> *There are some voices inside my head that are very critical of me,*
> *and I'll never get them to quiet down.*

— check out Step 2, Quiet the Inner Critic. You can quiet the chatter and learn to use affirmations to knock out the negative self-talk in your life with the positive!

If you checked off this one as "never" —

> *Sometimes I feel there's a happy person inside of me who wants to get out.*

— be sure to review Step 4, Connect with the Happy Person Inside. Even if you answered "sometimes" or "always" to this one, we will be connecting with the Happy Person Inside in that chapter, so get ready for some fun!

By filling out this survey, you now have a good idea of what exercises to pay close attention to as you go through this book. But I do suggest that you go through all the exercises in this book, as we'll touch on these areas many times in the book and you'll have many opportunities to work on what you need to do to move forward and thrive!

MOVING INTO THE FUTURE

Now let's look at the last two statements that you filled out on the survey.

First, **"If I could change one thing about my life, I'd..."**

Did writing about this give you any new insight into what may stand in the way of you moving on? For example, if you wrote —

I was so young when I had my kids. They've never appreciated me.

— I'd say that is a pretty limiting statement. First of all, right now you can't do much about the fact that you had your kids when you did. And second, you don't really have any control over whether your kids appreciate you or not. They may appreciate you more in the future, or they may not ever do so. All you can do is be the best mother you know how to be and let it go at that. What I've learned about a limiting statement like this is that all things happen for a reason. You may not know the reason right now that you had this experience (and you may never know), but you can learn and grow from it. See it as a gift, and seize the opportunity to think positive! Maybe when you get your life moving, your children will admire and appreciate you for that. Shifting your attitude about these things can make all the difference in your life.

If you wrote something like —

I regret not finishing school so I could get a good job and feel better about myself.

— talk about an opportunity knocking at your door! Who says you can't go back to school now? What is holding you back? When we get to Step 7, Set New Goals, we'll work more on that!

Second (my favorite): **If I had $10 million and all the time to do whatever I wanted to do, I'd...** I hope your answer to that was big! If there was ever a time in your life to think big, this is it!

Later in the book when we set new goals, we'll revisit what you wrote here, but for now, just notice if you wrote about any of the following:

- Did you use any of the money to help others and provide for your family and loved ones?
- Did you bring up some dream that you had long ago forgotten about and might want to think about again?
- Did you have fun with the idea that without the limitations that we usually use as excuses (no money, no time), you could do anything?

Hold on to this unlimited belief that anything is possible! There is much more in this book that will give you the feeling of limitless possibilities and bring you to a place where some of those possibilities can grow into realities. Savor the thought that you are on the brink of a new life and anything can happen. Let's finish with a list of unlimited beliefs for yourself. Let's see how they feel for you.

- I can create a new life for myself and avenge the abuse I have experienced.
- I can discover my inner wisdom and lower the negative voices in my life.
- I can tap into my truest desires and uncover my inner strengths.
- I can conquer my fears and embrace change.
- I can find meaningful work that I love and live the creative, active life that I long to lead.

These are actually more like "affirmations" — things you want to affirm that are true and possible in your life. Check off any that feel right for you and write an affirmation below about what you want to achieve for yourself in the course of reading this book. Then hold onto this good stuff! We'll use it all later in this book to help you on your glorious journey from victim to survivor to thriver!

MY AFFIRMATIONS: Write some now!

Living well is the best revenge!

After all, isn't getting on with one's life the most exacting revenge against those who have beaten us down and told us we are nothing?

But it is hard to face our stories! Can't you just hear the chatter — Why didn't you leave sooner? How could you be with such a man? What were you thinking? Then too, as a formerly abused woman, you may face costly ongoing legal battles with your abusive ex-partner on such issues as property division, child custody and child support. You may have substance abuse issues in your life as a result of the abuse or have little or no education or no job or a low-paying job and little financial backing or support from your family or friends. Your culture or religion may judge you about leaving a partner or marriage, even if your partner is abusive to you.

Yes, those voices keeping you down can be loud and convincing. *This is too hard*, you may tell yourself. *It's not going to work. I am a victim and will always be one. I don't deserve any better.*

You do have another voice inside you to listen to, however. That voice—strong, confident and untouched by all that has ever happen to you—is telling you to take the journey. Who says you can't find positive energy in life, follow your dreams, push through your fears and embrace the thriver spirit inside you?

Over the years, I have worked with hundreds of women who describe themselves as survivors of abuse. Each time I have given them the choice of reliving the abuse and the pain inflicted on them or reaching deep down inside to uncover their true heart's desires, they choose the latter. They have set goals for themselves that they have not only achieved but also have spurred them on to making bigger and better changes for themselves and their children. They have done, in many cases, what they have thought was unimaginable! They have reclaimed their lives after abuse and permanently broken the cycle of violence.

This book, with its "seven-step" format for thriving after abuse, offers you a chance to find the same "life-altering" experience that can bring new vigor and energy to your life. You can check out some of the women who share their thriver success stories later in this book. I hope these stories give you the inspiration and motivation you need to take the journey to wholeness, healing and recovery.

Finally, you may fear the possibility that you will return to an abusive relationship. Will you see the warning signs of abuse the next time around? Will a healthy, happy relationship ever come your way? That's a real fear! But don't worry! You can overcome all these obstacles and learn much, much more in this book about the journey to becoming a thriver.

So let's explore the seven steps we can use to make this amazing, transformational journey to find freedom, peace, wonder and joy in our lives!

SEVEN STEPS ON THE JOURNEY TO THRIVING AFTER ABUSE

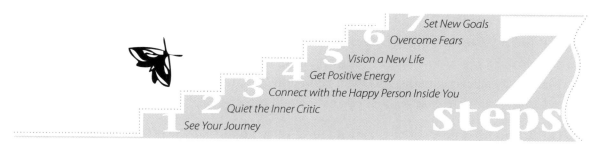

Set New Goals
Overcome Fears
Vision a New Life
Get Positive Energy
Connect with the Happy Person Inside You
Quiet the Inner Critic
See Your Journey

STEP 1: You'll see your journey by beginning with a writing exercise about your favorite fairy tales. These stories can help you see that in everyone's life there is a struggle of some kind (e.g., a loss of a job, divorce, illness, abuse, violence). That struggle can be overcome by a life-altering event (e.g., Cinderella meets the fairy godmother, Sleeping Beauty wakes up) that sets us on the road to the happy ending. No matter how many times I do this exercise with women, they always tell me they believe in the happy ending. It will be our work, then, to get you there… to the Happy Ending!

STEP 2: You'll quiet the Inner Critic, that negative voice in your head from childhood that becomes overprotective and too rigid for you as an adult. For abused women, that voice tells us we're no good, stupid, can't do anything right, and it can also be the voice of the abuser. With an interactive exercise, we will tune into the voice of our Inner Critic, learn to respond to it and create affirmations to help quiet its chatter and reduce its potency to sabotage or derail us on the way to our Happy Ending!

STEP 3: You'll connect with the Happy Person Inside You, a part of you that has probably been trounced down by the abuse in your life. She is the cheerleader inside who loves you, supports you and guides you with great wisdom if only you would listen.

STEP 4: You'll get the positive energy going again in your life by working with the energy of the Happy Person Inside you and shifting your focus to express gratitude for all the good things in your life — past, present and future!

STEP 5: You'll vision a new life for you and your children, beginning with focusing on what you are passionate about and what dreams and desires you may have given up on in your life. You'll look at what drives you to find the work you love, such as the search for meaningful work, the need to help others or make the world a better place. Then you'll work on manifesting what you desire. You can do it!

STEP 6: You'll overcome your fears and limiting beliefs, such as "Abuse has always been a part of my life. I can't do anything about it," or "Bad things always happen to me," or "There is no way I can create the life I want right now." You'll explore peak experiences in your livfe and identify positive patterns so you can repeat them again.

STEP 7: You'll set new short-term and long-term goals that will reflect the new, positive energy in your life and allow you to thrive, not merely survive the abuse. We'll look at dreams deferred, like going to law school, traveling around the world, writing a book, and we'll define simple, easy steps so you can attain goals without any more delay.

SEVEN STEPS GET RESULTS

Women who take the journey from victim to survivor to thriver are less likely to return to an abusive relationship or suffer the long-term physical and psychological consequences of the abuse they have experienced. It makes sense! Using the Seven Steps to Thriving After Abuse outlined in this book can produce significant, tangible changes in your life as it has in the lives of many other women—a noticeable change in attitude about the abuse and your belief in your ability to transform to your life.

Many women I have worked with have indicated in the survey that you filled out earlier that:

Abuse has always been in my life. I can't do much about it.
My biggest fear is that I'll never get my life together.
I'll never figure out who I am or what I want to be when I grow up.
There is no way I can create the life I want right now.

But after working with me on the seven-step approach, they report a shift in these attitudes and also in the belief that taking time for themselves is not a selfish thing to do. They are grateful to have finally found a group of women who have experienced abuse in the past and now want to move on with their lives.

Actually, I have seen all of these new unlimited beliefs be strengthened as women continue to work with me in a strong community of like-minded women and through it, the well-being and financial stability of these women has been greatly increased. Most importantly the women I have worked with have not returned to an abusive relationship, and several have entered new, healthy relationships, some for the first time in their lives.

These women have done amazing things! They have been spurred on to start their own businesses, return to school to get advanced degrees in law and medicine, get new jobs at higher pay that more closely matches to their skills and talents, resume singing careers and become first-time homeowners.

What these courageous journeys have taught me is that the truest measure of our lives is not what we have experienced but what we have made of our experiences. We don't really know how good it can get once we get positive and focus our energies on our future, not the past. Whatever we might have imagined for ourselves is only a fraction of what we can have when we free ourselves to live well, be happy and create the life we want.

Then living well is, in fact, our greatest revenge.

TAKE THE JOURNEY

Just as it may take a woman up to seven times to leave an abusive relationship, it may also take several tries for you to reclaim your life after abuse. Each time, the greatest barrier that may keep you from moving on is that you don't feel positive about yourself and your future life.

The seven-step approach in this book can help you take this journey as someone who has been abused or violated in her life. Others may also find this book and its approach of value, including:

Family, friends and coworkers of women who have been abused: Often the family, friends and loved ones of women who have been abused want to help, but they don't know how. This book is not only a way for them to learn about and understand the recovery process, but also would be a great gift idea for a friend or family member to show them that they care.

Staff of shelters and crisis centers: According to the National Coalition on Domestic Violence, there are 2,000 domestic violence shelters in the United States and 1,000 sexual assault crisis centers. In these programs, there are hundreds of advocate and counselors who work with thousands of women who are survivors of abuse or sexual assault every year. These workers routinely look for new approaches to help these women move beyond the violence, and many of the techniques in this book could be easily adapted for use in group or individual counseling sessions.

Counselors and therapists who work with these women: According to the American Association for Marriage and Family Therapy, there are more than 50,000 marriage and family therapists treating individuals, couples and families nationwide. The National Association of Social Workers (NASW), the largest membership organization of professional social workers in the world, has 153,000 members. The American Psychological Association (APA), with more than 150,000 members, is the largest association of psychologists. Many of these marriage and family therapists, social workers and psychologists provide individual and group therapy for women who have experienced abuse, trauma or violence. While this book is not intended to be a substitute for therapy, it does provide therapists with practical exercises and creative techniques to help patients set new goals for their lives and heal from past trauma and abuse.

Attorneys, doctors and other professional caregivers: These professionals are always looking for resources and materials to share with clients and patients. This book is a way to help women move beyond traumatic divorces, custody battles and illnesses or physical injuries either caused by the abuser or the stress of the situation. Other caregivers who could use the book are clergy, child welfare workers, school counselors and nurses.

Whether you are taking the journey yourself or helping another to do so, let's embrace this amazing, life-affirming process now and create a brilliant new future for ourselves and our children.

Take the journey today. Transformation awaits!

> ***Just when the caterpillar thought the world was***
> ***over, it became a butterfly.***
>
> — PROVERB

Take the first step in faith. You don't have to see the whole staircase, just take the first step.

– MARTIN LUTHER KING

Step 1
See Your Journey

*I*f I have learned anything over the last fifteen years working with hundreds of women who have been abused and from dealing with the violent, senseless death of my niece Maggie, it is that we are all on a journey in this lifetime. The first step is to see the journey, know that it is a journey of spirit and that it can help us find ourselves and our purpose in this lifetime.

What a journey to celebrate!

But before I take you through an exercise that can help you see your journey, it is important for us to move into another part of our brain—the amazing part where our creativity, intuition and deepest feelings lie.

LETTING OUR RIGHT BRAINS COME OUT TO PLAY

We live in a culture that is very left-brained. In it, we have to be logical and rational, deal with facts, make decisions and worry about being perfect and doing the right thing.

But there is a warmer, fuzzier part of us. It is the right side of our brains where we are emotional, sensual and spontaneous. That hemisphere of the brain holds our creative, playful selves. We can see that side most easily by watching children, particularly at a very young age, be very open and much more accessible and tuned into the right side of their brains. You can see it as they play, imagine and create. It is a wonderful, exciting thing, and it makes them free and unlimited.

If you have been abused or assaulted, the left side of your brain has probably needed to take over for a while. It was there to help you figure out how to get help and make decisions about where you would live so that you and your children could be safe. Once you are out of the situation, however, you need to rejuvenate and reenergize yourself with something that takes you back to your right brain. It's hard to envision a new life free of abuse, pain and violence if you aren't tuned into the creative, intuitive right-brain part of yourself. Accessing that side of the brain is essential if you want to take the journey, described earlier in this book, from victim to survivor to thriver. It is a journey of spirit, one that can transform your life, and I think you are ready for it!

The exercises in this section are designed to help start you on this amazing journey, but I will warn you that moving into the right side of the brain may feel new or funny to you at first. You may not clearly remember being there before or how to get back there again. For example, we access that part of us every day in our dreams, but often we don't understand the pictures and stories that come to us there as they tap into our creative unconscious, and we wake up confused and unenlightened.

Don't get frustrated if you have trouble with this right-brained thing right away. I, myself, am very left-brained. I have always been analytical, logical and able to solve problems. As an attorney, I was trained to think and act in my left brain, but as a writer, I have had to learn to access my right brain, as it is there that the creative process begins. On my journey to thriver, I have had to access that right hemisphere of my brain because it has the vision, feelings and intuition I needed to get me started on my new path.

Let's start with a list showing the differences between the right and left brain.

LEFT BRAIN	RIGHT BRAIN
Speaks in Words	Loves Images, Lives in Fantasies
Keeps Order, Makes Lists, Result-Oriented	Creates Freely, Takes Risks
Logical, Analytical	Lives in a World of Feelings and Emotions
Thinking, Informative, Decisive	Insightful, Intuitive
Demands Accuracy, Perfection	Is Sensuous, Seeks Pleasure and Joy

Notice how the left brain deals very much in facts, decisions and actions. It is methodical and brings order to our world. We want and need the left brain in our lives. It helps us organize ourselves and gets us from one place to another. But we also need the right brain to give us entrée to the creative unconscious, that part of us that creates freely, loves images and is playful and spontaneous.

For a simple example, your left brain may have led you to the advertisement or the person who recommended that you buy this book. But it was your right brain that immediately connected to something about this book, maybe the title or the cover art, something intuitive that let you know that this book was for you.

While you want to tap into your right brain as much as possible, living there all the time is too chaotic and overwhelming for anyone. What you want to do is strike a balance between these two hemispheres of the brain. You want to engage the right brain to help you vision, create and be spontaneous, then use the left brain to put order to the vision and set the goals and objectives you need to get yourself there.

That's exactly how we'll work in this book. We'll do both kinds of exercises, but for now let's start with one that gives you some idea, image or feeling of what the left brain means when it uses the words "right brain." Remember, the left brain has the words or language for what we experience in the right brain. But these experiences don't begin as a word or articulation in our left brain. They begin as an image, feeling or abstraction in the right brain and get translated in the left brain into a word or phrase that best describes the experience, although sometimes very inadequately. So let's do a quick exercise to get in touch with the times that we made contact with our right brain and its amazing qualities.

THE EXERCISE: MOVING INTO THE RIGHT BRAIN

First, think about something that makes you really happy. You know, that giddy, silly, lighthearted feeling of doing something you really love to do. For me, it's going to the movies. I love the way I feel when I go into a theater and the lights go down and the screen is filled up with a story that I lose myself in until the lights go back up. In those few hours, I am totally in my right brain absorbing all the images on the movie screen. As I do, all my problems fade away, and I feel really reenergized when I leave.

What kinds of activities give you that kind of feeling? They don't have to be big events or very complicated. I get the same feeling from riding my bike, reading a good book, sitting by the ocean, having dinner with friends or walking in my neighborhood.

Writing from a prompt here, let's make a quick list of activities you love to do.

(Remember, prompts can help you start writing. Don't worry that you'll do this wrong or think about it too much.)

✒ **PROMPT:** I feel happy, relaxed, joyful, when I am —

In your journal or notebook, draw lines to create three columns.

Then make a list of those activities in Column 1. After each one of these activities, make a note in Column 2 — How often do you do this? And in Column 3 — When was the last time you did it?

For example, I'd note on my list:

ACTIVITY	HOW OFTEN?	LAST TIME I DID IT
Going to the movies	twice a month	last month
Riding my bike	weekly in summer	last fall
Reading a good book	nightly before bed	two nights ago
Sitting by the ocean	every so often	two weeks ago

Take a look at your list.

First, are you doing the things that you love that take you into the right brain often enough? Looking at my list, maybe I should be going to the movies more than twice a month if they make me so happy and connect me to that special part of me. Or perhaps I should plan a regular time to go sit by the ocean, which I love to do.

Second, pick out one or two activities that you haven't done for a while. Make a plan in the next day or two to do them. Don't procrastinate. Do them now!

When you do, take the time to write down how you felt before, during and after the activity. Be more aware, for example, of what almost stopped you from doing the activity, what it felt like while you were doing it and how great you felt afterwards.

For example, for me, sitting by the ocean...

BEFORE — I FEEL OR TELL MYSELF: I really don't have time to do this. It's too far for me to travel. I really don't need to do it. I don't want to waste the gas.

DURING — I FEEL OR TELL MYSELF: Gosh, this does feel really nice. I can feel myself relaxing. It takes me away from my problems and troubles. Water has a calming effect on me. I like being here. I have made a good choice. Why didn't I come here sooner?

AFTER — I FEEL OR TELL MYSELF: That was great! I'm going to do that again soon. I feel so energized, so happy, so positive about everything in my life. I can take it all on now. What a great gift this is for me! I love how I am feeling so creative. New thoughts are coming now. I have a plan for dealing with things I couldn't handle before. This is the best thing I've done for myself in a long time.

Record some of your BEFORE, DURING and AFTER feelings in your journal or notebook when you do one of the activities you selected from your list.

✎ **PROMPT:** Before

✎ **PROMPT:** During

✎ **PROMPT:** After

Wow! Isn't this great! Look what this simple activity has done for you!

You have connected for a short period of time, maybe even just a few seconds, with the fabulous feeling of being in the right side of your brain. Don't you want to do that some more? You can! We'll be going into the right brain throughout this workbook, and each time you do, you'll feel closer to a place that makes you feel amazing. Moreover, you will learn how easy it is to go there more often and stay in that feeling for longer periods of time. It is, in some way, as simple as sounding the way we feel. As children we have little difficulty doing that. We squealed with delight when we opened our presents on Christmas morning, we were so sad when our pet goldfish died, we were silly when we had a pillow fight at a slumber party and happy when we had an ice-cream cone as a treat for doing well in school. Reaching back to those childlike feelings is one way of describing how it feels when we make contact with the right side of our brain. It is the place we feel happy, safe and joyous. Perhaps these are words or concepts that you have not been in contact with for a long time, or maybe you've never really felt them at all.

Come on the journey to the right side of the brain. Do it now! You really can't wait any longer to go to that wondrous, fantastic place. You can do it!

Now that you are in the glorious right brain, let's explore together the first step on your journey to thriving through the magical world of fairy tales.

FAIRY TALES CAN COME TRUE

When I was a little girl, I loved to read fairy tales.

Cinderella was my favorite. I loved what fairy tales had to offer — everything was magical and everyone lived happily ever after. Have you ever wondered why so few of us can make magic happen and find our own happy endings?

For women who have lived through abuse, it is hard for us to imagine that we can create the life we want or that fairy tales can indeed come true. But they can. I believe that each of us has an inner road map that can lead us to our happy ending. We just have to discover that path and go there!

Here's how to begin. Think of your favorite fairy tale. Do this quickly! Pick one that delighted you as a child and still makes you smile. You may be a Cinderella girl like me or maybe you liked Sleeping Beauty, Snow White and the Seven Dwarfs or Hansel and Gretel.

If you don't have a favorite fairy tale, think of a favorite children's story like the Wizard of Oz, Alice in Wonderland or Jack in the Bean Stalk. If you don't have one of those, think of a favorite book, movie or the story of a person you admire, like Oprah Winfrey or Mother Teresa.

THE EXERCISE: HONORING OUR STORIES

✎ **PROMPT:** Write the name of your favorite story in your journal or notebook.

Now do a five-minute "free write" about this story from the two prompts on the next page. (For more on writing from prompts, review "How to Use This Book" on page 3.)

REMEMBER! There are no rules! You can't do this wrong!

✎ **PROMPT:** I love this story because:

✎ **PROMPT:** Lessons I have learned from this story are:

Here's what I have written about the Cinderella story:

I love the story of Cinderella because — it makes me feel that no matter what happens, I can survive. Cinderella lost her mother, and then her father married Cinderella's cruel stepmother. When her father died, she became a servant, but Cinderella didn't get angry or bitter. One day her fairy godmother magically transformed Cinderella's rags into a beautiful gown so that she could go to the ball. I love how she discovered the "Prince Charming" inside her, and once she was transformed, she attracted someone who was just as wonderful as she was.

The lesson that I learned — from the Cinderella story is never give up. No matter how hard your life is, magical things can happen. Being happy is the most important thing, and making other people happy is the second. In my story of Cinderella, she invites her stepmother and sisters to live with her and her Prince. They all live happily ever after.

In writing about your favorite story, did you get the same "journey" as I did from the Cinderella story?

This journey begins with struggle — loss, abuse and major challenges. Like Cinderella, we all have parts of our lives filled with trials, tribulation and trauma. For a woman who has been abused, these events can be life-threatening, humiliating, degrading, frightening, painful and feel like they will never end. But in everyone's journey, there is a moment of transformation, when, like Cinderella, a "fairy godmother" shows up and we can see that all is indeed possible. Then we can push through our fears, even physical fears, to get to our happy ending.

VICTIM TO SURVIVOR TO THRIVER!

Yes, there is a happy ending! It is in the amazing journey from VICTIM to SURVIVOR to THRIVER!

The words in each column below describe the experience of each stage of this journey from **Struggle** to **Transformation** to the **Happy Ending**. Remember: it's easy to get stuck in the victim/struggle stage. There, we may experience anger, depression, hopelessness, doubt, fear and despair. But as survivors, and ultimately thrivers, we can move beyond victim to our own happy endings!

STRUGGLE	TRANSFORMATION	THE HAPPY ENDING
Abuse	Magic	Hope
Pain	Awaken	Unconditional Love
Evil	Never Give Up	Peace
Sickness	Persistence	Freedom
Death	Determination	Security
Unhappiness	Pride	Healthy
Bad	Self-Care	Self-Love
Cruel	Soothing	Joy
Obstacles	Change	Home
Suffering	Courageous	Positive
Ugly	Empowerment	Abundance
	Nurturing	Family
Anger	Forgiveness	Friends
Depressed	Assertive	Complete
Hopelessness	Dream	Whole
Doubt	Patience	Strong
Despair	Simplify	Eternal
Fear	Diversity	Happy
	Shared	Satisfied
		Ecstatic
VICTIM	**SURVIVOR**	**THRIVER**

Now, what lessons have you learned from your favorite fairy tale or story? Here are some that I've gotten from the stories mentioned above:

"Don't give up, Cinderella."

"Sleeping Beauty will wake up."

"A little organized chaos like Alice in Wonderland where down is up and up is down will help me create the life I want."

Here's what Sherry, a woman I have worked with, wrote about the lesson she learned from Beauty and the Beast:

Belle, the princess, wants to be her own person without being controlled and to be loved for who she is. She wants to be free to make her own choices and have her own dreams. Beast loves her not only for her beauty, but also for who she is on the inside. In the end, he transforms into her true love, her handsome prince. The lesson to be learned is that it is not what is on the outside that matters most; it is what is on the inside that counts. That is person's true self. We must remember that looks can be deceiving, and beauty lies within.

THE STRUGGLE

Now let's reframe the telling of your own real-life story, given what you have learned about the journey from your favorite story. You might see that you've been living your own happy ending right now and didn't even know it! Tell this part of the story quickly, avoiding what might depress or make you angry. These are emotions for another day. Write about the obstacles you faced and how you overcame them. You are the heroine of your own story!

✎ **PROMPT:** Write down this part of your journey in your journal or notebook.

THE TRANSFORMATION

This part of the story is when you realized you were being abused and decided to do something about it. There is great power in that moment! It is an "AH-HA!" moment when you know that you can only go forward with your life, not back. Perhaps working through this book will be that kind of moment for you. I hope so. Here are some words to describe this part of the journey: "hope," "change," "renewed spirit" and "magic." Use these and others to write about how you felt in your moment of transformation, when you knew you had to move on.

✎ **PROMPT:** Write down this part of your journey in your journal or notebook.

THE HAPPY ENDING

This is the fun part that describes what you've been yearning for. Make it BIG. Make it NOW!

✎ **PROMPT:** Write down this part of your journey in your journal or notebook.

There you have it! Your life as a fairy tale coming true!

Here's what Kathy, a woman I have worked with, wrote for this exercise:

I was finally able to put my ex-partner behind me and move on. I gathered my strength and my determination, and I let go — the hardest thing of all for me. I've been able to heal and to create the life I want to live. I have made so many cherished friends, and my life is filled with love, discovery, laughter and joyous serenity.

I found my true career path and am doing the work that I've always felt an inner compulsion to do. I wake up every morning and look forward with eagerness and anticipation to the work I will do that day. I have been able to obtain a job that gives me a viable income and do the work I have come to this life to do. I feel satisfaction and deep fulfillment because I am no longer going through the motions and am working in a creative job that allows my spirit to be released and sing its song.

My life is now free of constant worry, fear and anxiety. I travel the world as I've always longed to do. I have found peace and contentment in all the blessings which surround me — my son, my family, my friends, my work, my treasured books, music and nature, my spirituality. I am whole and complete.

So now that I have you believing that fairy tales can come true, you are ready to step into the vision of how you, too, can take the magical journey from victim to survivor to thriver. There is a great life waiting for you, and you deserve it!

Be the princess in your own fairy tale and make your dreams come true!

Happily ever after isn't a fairy tale.
It's a choice.

— FAWN WEAVER

You are bigger than the demons you have imagined. You'll outlast them. You always have.

– MARIANNE WILLIAMSON

Step 2
Quiet the Inner Critic

nside us is a voice that constantly criticizes and finds fault with all we do. I call that the "Inner Critic," and at times it can be nasty and mean. The Inner Critic usually comes from a voice in our childhood when our parents said things like:

"Don't touch the stove. It's hot!"

"Look both ways when you cross the street."

"Don't play with matches. You'll burn the house down!"

These protective messages were meant to teach us to take care of ourselves, but as we grew up that voice began to dictate all the "shoulds" in our lives. Its ramblings often sound like this:

"You should have taken that job. You are a failure."

"You should be a better mother."

"Your kids are a mess."

"Why can't you find someone nice to marry?"

The Inner Critic fuels our fears and insecurities and blocks us from taking positive, creative risks in our lives. It is very clever and knows exactly how to get to us. For some women who have been abused, the Inner Critic can take on the voice of the abusive person. It says *"You will never make it alone," "You are fat and stupid"* or *"You deserve to be beaten."*

We can't stop the chatter of the Inner Critic inside our heads. Such negative self-talk will always be with us. But we can turn it down, just as you can turn down the volume on your television set or radio.

THE EXERCISE: FACING THE INNER CRITIC

Here's an exercise to quiet even the most fierce Inner Critic. Take a moment to close your eyes and let yourself hear the critical voice inside your head.

It may be a voice from your childhood — your mother or father or a teacher — and it may be male or female. Let it speak about your life for a moment without blocking out what it says.

Now open your eyes, and draw a line down the page of your journal or notebook.

PROMPT: Write down in the left-hand column a list of your Inner Critic's chatter. Perhaps it is a word, a phrase or a simple sentence.

Whatever it is saying, let it rip and put it on the page!

Read the list aloud, then close your eyes again and listen for any more to add.

When you are done, take a deep breath, close your eyes and let that voice go.

PROMPT: Write in the right-hand column a response to each thing your Inner Critic said.

Be strong, affirming and positive in your responses. You can be feisty too, like "Who cares?" or "Not true!" If your Inner Critic wrote, "You're a bad mother," your response is "I'm a great mother." Respond to each remark until your list looks like the one below. Even if your Inner Critic is saying so, you can't do this wrong!

INNER CRITIC	YOUR RESPONSE
I'm fat, stupid and ugly.	*I am beautiful just the way I am.*
I deserve to be treated badly.	*No one deserves to be abused.*
Nobody has ever really loved me.	*I am loved and lovable!*
I'm not good enough.	*I am enough!*
I'm wasting my time.	*My time is my own.*
I should be cleaning my house!	*Housework can wait!*
I'm a failure. I never do anything right.	*I am perfect as I am.*

What have we learned here? We do have a response to every one of the Inner Critic's crippling criticisms and discouraging comments. Know that this negative voice is not the truth about your life; it's only one view, and it is your choice to see your life as positive or negative. As Eleanor Roosevelt said, "No one can make you feel inferior without your consent."

If you are in the victim or struggle part of your journey (See Step 1, See Your Journey), the Inner Critic will be very loud and try hard to convince you how lousy your life is and how nothing good ever comes your way.

If you feel like a survivor, the voice will be less loud and not quite so convincing. You may respond, "But I survived" and "Good things come from bad."

In the thriver stage, the voice is all but drowned out. You are strong and your response is immediate. "I am somebody! I'm going somewhere!"

Since positive attracts positive into your life and negative brings negative, you want to stay in that positive place, thinking positive thoughts. Like magnets, we attract what is most like ourselves. As one of the women in my workshops put it, "Happy things happen to happy people." Or as Oprah Winfrey has said, "The more you praise and celebrate your life, the more there is to praise."

Use this exercise whenever you need to spend some time with your Inner Critic. Don't be afraid to find out what it is saying about you and your life. At first, it may feel like you are putting too much focus on the negative, but you do want to know what the Inner Critic is saying. You need to remind yourself regularly that you do have a response to everything it puts out, so why not be prepared to combat its limiting beliefs and negative comments? That's the only way to quiet it down and tame it for good.

WRITING AFFIRMATIONS

One way to quiet the Inner Critic is to create affirmations about you and your life. Read down the right-hand column of your list of positive responses on previous page to the Inner Critic's remarks. Are there any affirming statements that particularly speak to you?

Looking back at my sample, there are several great affirmations:

I am loved and lovable.   *I am becoming the person I truly want to be.*
I am beautiful just the way I am.   *I am perfect as I am.*

Here's more from some of the women I have worked with:

I am a beautiful person.   *I have something.*
I'm going somewhere!   *I am taking care of myself.*
I am making good choices.   *I am my true self.*
I am whole and complete.   *I am strong and courageous.*
I am powerful.   *I am worthy of love and friendship.*

These are called "affirmations" because they are affirming something that is true about us in the most positive way at the present time. You wouldn't say in an affirmation "I'm trying to take care of myself," rather "I am healthy and happy." It's not that "I will be somebody someday", it is "I am somebody today."

Affirmations can also be statements that you can grow into, something to challenge and stretch you into what you truly want to become. One affirmation that you may not be able to feel today but could move into is "I am a thriver." Let yourself feel your energy going in that direction each time you say those words.

Get a large, thick black marker or crayon and write some of your affirmations on pieces of paper that you display around your house. Put some on your bathroom mirror so that you see them every morning or on your computer monitor so you look at them often. You can also post the goals and affirmations you came up with earlier in the Introduction section of this book.

Believe in your affirmations! Go BIG with them and get strong! When you have outgrown them, make some new ones that will stretch you even further on this journey from victim to survivor to thriver.

> *Beware of allowing a tactless word, a rebuttal, a*
> *rejection to obliterate the whole sky.*
>
> — Anais Nin

*Joy is what happens
to us when we
allow ourselves to
recognize how good
things really are.*

– MARIANNE WILLIAMSON

Step 3
Connect with the Happy Person Inside You

here is a Happy Person Inside You just waiting to get out! She is the thriver energy inside you, and she is thrilled to see that we are going to be talking a lot about her in this book. She is jumping off the page right now! She is the warm, fuzzy part of you that is happy and carefree. You may have lost contact with that part of yourself entirely, but she is ready to come play with you now and can't wait for the fun to begin.

Remember that great positive energy we got when we responded to the Inner Critic in Step 2? That's the energy to be in as you do this next exercise. The Inner Critic is gone, banished by the Happy Person Inside You, who, of course, wrote those wonderful responses to the mean, nasty Inner Critic. Now that you are in contact with her, close your eyes and feel that energy go through you.

THE EXERCISE: WRITING A "HAPPY PERSON" LETTER

When you are ready, I want you to write a letter to yourself from the Happy Person Inside You. Here's the way to start. Don't hold back! Let it be big!

✍ **PROMPT:** Write a letter to yourself in your journal or notebook.

Dear _____ (insert your name)

I Am the Happy Person Inside You and I Want to Tell You Something...

She is your best cheerleader and she loves you, loves you, loves you unconditionally! She has great wisdom to share with you. Make it big and bold!

WOW! Wasn't that great? Now read aloud what you have written. You need to get this wondrous, happy, strong, wise voice out into the Universe.

I bet what you wrote was very positive and very supportive of you and where you are *now*. Of course it was! The Happy Person Inside You thinks you are a fabulous person doing fabulous things! She is there for you always, no matter what. She knows you so well because she is you, the best side of you — the thriver in you — and you want to maintain contact with her. We'll ask her later in this book to help you envision a future for yourself and your children that is truly wonderful.

The Happy Person Inside You is the immortal part of you, the part that never dies. She is your spirit, your soul, your Inner Guide, the Divine, God — whatever you choose to call her — and she loves you. Now that you have found a way to talk to her, keep it up. Ask her for a gift. See if she has a pet name for you. Ask her to guide you through a tough decision you may be making right now. Confide in her! Trust her! She is perfect! She is YOU!

On the next page are samplings of what women I have worked with have written for this exercise. I share these with you so that you can get more of the energy of this Happy Person Inside You. But don't let your Inner Critic creep in when you read these pieces. No matter what you wrote above, you did not do it wrong! How could you? The Happy Person Inside You is perfect. She is YOU!

When you are finished reading these samples, have the Happy Person Inside You write you a follow-up letter. Ask her to tell you how to stay in contact with her. Promise her you will. This is what you need and deserve!

I AM THE HAPPY PERSON INSIDE YOU AND I WANT TO TELL YOU SOMETHING...

You are the most beautiful radiant bright star that glows from deep in your heart. You give that light to this Universe in such a loving and unselfish way that makes you so special to this lifetime. You are my beloved and most cherished, and I give you my love infinitely to support and fulfill you in every way with endless supply. I am always there for you even when you don't choose to see me, so never worry because I will be here forever and ever. — MARY

I miss you. Can you come out to play? I have a great idea for us. Let's travel north and make new and pleasant memories together. Let's swim across a lake as far as we can. I'll hold you up when you get tired because I'm very strong and able. Don't bring a watch or money with you, because there is no price for our time together. I love you! — HEATHER

You are a caring, smart, wonderful person. You just need to lighten up on yourself. Enjoy yourself more. Play with your dollhouse again. Pay attention to your teddy bears! You didn't survive all that you did just to be in a rut and be miserable. You were meant to be happy — so enjoy life! — GAYLENE

Every time you play those polka tapes, I love to polka dance with you. It makes us so happy. All of the wishes and hopes you have are going to happen. You and I together, one day at a time, can make this become a reality. Don't be discouraged if you slip back into the victim role. It is just a thought. Think of something beautiful and loving like yourself. You deserve to have all the positive things in your life. Together we can make it happen. I love you! — LINDA

You are a very caring person. You have so much potential with so much to give. You have a calming manner and a lovely smile. It's amazing how much you've done with your life. You have many years ahead of you to enjoy. It's never too late. Remember what is important: self-love, your wonderful man, and a family of friends. I love you. — ROBIN

You have such a great smile that lights up your eyes, and your face beams. You make someone else smile. You have the biggest heart. You are caring. You listen to other people's problems and help people. You have a lot to offer. Know your boundaries. Don't overstep them! You like to leave them laughing. You love nature. You inhale life moment by moment. God made Earth like paintings — the oceans, mountains, rivers and forests. — CHRISTINE

You are a wonderful person to know and to love. You are kind and generous to others and very giving of your time. You have a kind heart and a gentle soul few people ever truly know. Now be kind to yourself. You have the right to be happy in this life, so give yourself the time you need to be the person you are meant to be, to fulfill the dreams you always dream. Believe in yourself, and you can do anything you want to do. Be free to be who you are. Everything else will fall into place as it is meant to. I love you. I am you. — KATHY

Remember all your strengths. You have incredible compassion for so many. May you grant yourself this same compassion. All your experiences have given you strength and fortitude. Without these experiences, you would not be the person you are today. Although painful in nature, they molded you into who you are today. Let your friends be your cheerleaders as you start down the road and also the ones who are your safety net should you stumble and fall. The love and compassion you feel for others will help you continue. Embrace yourself and all that you are. Stand tall against the storms. Embrace the warmth of the sun. Know that you are where you are supposed to be. Let go. Begin anew. — LINDA

I am thrilled to visit with you today. I enjoy your company, listening to your stories and sharing mine. You are a great friend, and I love having fun with you. I have missed you for a while, but it feels so good to rekindle our relationship. I look forward to being with you and creating positive, memorable experiences. Let's do arts and crafts, collecting anything, outdoor fun, indoor activities. Music, dancing, food, travel and vacations, working with children, volunteering. Whenever you need me, wherever you are, I am only a whisper away. I don't care if you wake me up in the middle of the night. Why? Because I love you so much and you are special to me. I am truly blessed to know you and to have you in my life. Love always, the Happy Person Inside You! P.S. See you soon. — DARLENE

Let yourself have it and enjoy!
If you want to be happy, be.

— LEO TOLSTOY

The most powerful thing
you can do to change
the world is to change
your own beliefs about
the nature of life, people
and reality to something
more positive ...and begin
to act accordingly."

— SHAKTI GAWAIN

Step 4
Get Positive Energy

There is a thriver inside you who is just waiting to get out. She is the Happy Person Inside You, and she is fabulous!

We know she is there because in Step 3 we made contact with her, and the letter she wrote us was amazing! Remember what great wisdom she had about our lives and such positive, hopeful thoughts for our futures? She is our strongest advocate and best cheerleader. She loves us very much and wants us to do well.

Each time we make contact with this part of us that is thriving, we are truly living our Happy Ending, the one we explored previously in the fairy-tale exercise. But we don't have to wait until some time in the future to tap into the best part of our lives. The best part of our lives can be right now — if we can get the thriver in us to come out and stay out in full force!

Can you imagine how that would feel? To me, it would feel like coming home to a place that is easy and peaceful. A place where all is well and possible, where I have no doubts, fears or longing. From there, all unfolds as it should. When I lose contact with that strong, positive part of me, I can easily get lost, scared, confused and feel very alone. My world comes apart, and I am separated from what is good, kind and loving, not only to others, but also to myself.

When we love ourselves and extend loving-kindness to ourselves, we can easily give the same to others. In the Buddhist tradition, there is a practice that is called a loving-kindness or "metta" meditation. (See the Resources section for more information on this topic.) In this meditation, you use phrases like: "May I be safe. May I be healthy. May I be happy. May I be peaceful" — first about yourself, and then with others in your life, including those who you may not like or have issues with.

I often use this kind of meditation to get myself in a good frame of mind about my life. It helps me clear my mind of resentful thoughts and bad feelings about myself and others. I use it to remind myself that they, like me, have good intentions, even though we don't always convey what we intend in a clear way because our behaviors might suggest otherwise. Meditation is certainly one way to get in touch with yourself and clear your mind from all the millions of thoughts — positive and negative — that bombard you every day. I once heard meditation described as a way of moving into the space between our thoughts, where our minds can rest and our spirits can soar.

I like that idea and often use meditation as a way to reenergize myself. But even with meditation, the trick still is to stay in the thriver place, focused on the present and on what is positive and good about our lives and our futures for as long as we can every day. In this chapter, I want to introduce you to several exercises that I have used successfully to keep my own life moving forward with positive energy. With them, I have been able not merely to survive all the difficult things that have happened to me, including the violent and tragic death of my niece, Maggie, but I have able to thrive and transform myself in many ways.

OPENING UP TO POSITIVE ENERGY IN OUR LIVES

I have gotten better and better at taking this journey to thriving, so now I can go from making contact with the Happy Person Inside Me for a few minutes each day to spending whole days, weeks and even months in her wondrous company. In fact, what I have found is that the journey to our Happy Ending is a very instinctive one. But usually when something really good happens to us, we think we are just lucky or that the stars in the heavens have lined up for once. Or if we see someone else getting what she wanted, we think that somehow she is special or has some "in" with the powers that be. However, the process of making our dreams come true is how the Universe works, and the sooner we learn how to use it more consciously, the sooner we will be living our Happy Ending every single moment of our lives.

Enough talk about it. Let's do it! Let's invite pure, positive energy into our lives. As women who have been abused, we are more familiar with the energy of the "victim" part of our lives. That energy is fueled by negative thoughts and emotions like anger, depression, resentment, sadness. Sometimes we can feel more positive energy when we move from "victim" to "survivor," but often women go through life always being the victim and spending all their energy merely surviving each new difficulty in their lives. Their mantra becomes "I can survive anything," and so they do, but they never really thrive.

Remember our working definition of a thriver:

A thriver is a happy, self-confident and productive individual who believes she has a prosperous life ahead of her. She is primed to follow her dreams, go back to school, find a new job, start her own business or write her story. She believes in herself and in her future so much that she will not return to an abusive relationship. She speaks knowledgeably and confidently about her experiences and is not stuck in her anger or need for revenge. Living well is her best revenge!

Notice all those positive words to describe the thriver energy — we feel happy, confident, productive and prosperous. For women who have been abused and violently assaulted, going into and staying in this kind of positive energy may be very hard, but it can be done. In this chapter, we will concentrate on how to bring positive energy and emotion into our lives.

Remember, we make a choice to stay in our positive thoughts or our negative ones. When we did the Inner Critic exercise in Step 2, it was the simple choice of staying in the left-hand column of our Inner Critic's view of our lives or in the right-hand column where positive energy was flowing. We'll work more in this chapter about how to keep choosing to be positive and move forward.

Let's remember some of the words the Happy Person Inside You used in the sample writings in Step 3:

Beautiful	**Radiant**	**Glowing**	**Loving**	**Deserving**
Wonderful	**Smart**	**Graceful**	**Free**	**Powerful**
Good	**Strong**	**Happy**	**Creative**	**Pure Joy**

You can also add words from the Happy Person Inside's letter to you.

Make your THRIVER LIST of positive words that describe that energy in you now in your journal or notebook.

Great! Now let's do some more exploring. Here's a quick survey for you to complete so you can see what is of value and importance to you and the Happy Person Inside You.

WHAT IS IMPORTANT TO YOU?

From the list below, choose the things that are most important to you in your life and work.

RANK THEM AS: *#1 — Most Important — Absolutely Must Have*
#2 — Less Important — Nice to Have
#3 — Least Important — Don't Need

___ ✿   Making the World More Beautiful

___ ✿   Accomplishing Something

___ ✿   Having a Good Balance Between Work and Play

___ ✿   Being Liked

___ ✿   Getting Ahead in My Career

___ ✿   Working Well with My Coworkers

___ ✿   Having Good Friends

___ ✿   Being Creative

___ ✿   Doing Meaningful Work

___ ✿   Making a Difference

___ ✿   Doing Good Work, Excellence

___ ✿   Having Low Stress

___ ✿   Having Power

___ ✿   Helping or Healing Others

___ ✿   Having Integrity, Always Doing the Right Thing

___ ✿   A Good Salary

___ ✿   Making Sure My Children Are Well Prepared for Life

___ ✿   Finding What Will Make Me Happy

___ ✿   Being Independent

___ ✿   Being Intellectually Challenged in My Work

___ ✿   Learning New Things, Adding New Skills

___ ✿   Having a Pleasant Work Environment

___ ✿   Having a Lot of Status, Prestige

___ ✿   Being Recognized and Valued for What I Do by My Boss and Coworkers

___ ✿   Having Financial Security

___ ✿   Feeling Good About Myself and My Life

___ ✿   Providing for Myself and My Children

___ ✿   Taking Care of Myself

___ ✿   Having a Good Family Life

THE EXERCISE: CHOOSING WHAT'S IMPORTANT TO YOU

Let's take a look at the items that you ranked as #1 on the list of what is most important to you. If you have more than three items marked #1, see if you can narrow it down to only three.

✍ **PROMPT:** Write your top three #1 items from the survey in your journal or notebook.

Let's see what those choices might mean for you.

Say you had the following items listed as your top #1s —

Accomplishing Something • Doing Meaningful Work • Helping or Healing Others

— I would say your thriver is into finding a caring community and meaningful work that helps and serves others.

If your list looked more like this —

Having a Good Balance between Work and Play • Making Sure My Children Are Well Prepared for Life • Having a Good Family Life

— I would say that your thriver is invested in having family and friends that teach and practice unconditional love.

Finally, if your list included —

Doing Good Work, Excellence • Making a Difference • Having Integrity, Always Doing the Right Thing

— Integrity and Excellence excites the thriver in you.

What you also can get from this exercise is what the thriver is *not* interested in. Here's an example:

If you put these items as #3 —

Getting Ahead in My Career • Having a Lot of Status and Prestige • Having Financial Security • Having Power • Being Liked

— I'd say you are a person whose thriver is interested in more than financial success, gaining power or getting ahead just to get ahead.

Most women who I have worked with who have been abused or controlled in their lives will pick one or more of these items as a #3. In some cases, a woman who has been in an abusive, controlling relationship is least likely to be interested in having power or measuring her success by external factors, like how much money or status she has. On the other hand, I have also had women pick "Having Power" as a #2 or even a #1 item because, for the first time in their lives, they have the sense that they are finally coming into their power. Those women are most likely to have also chosen as a #1 or #2 "Being Independent," "Finding What Makes Me Happy" or "Feeling Good About Myself and My Life."

Let's look at the words that best describe the thriver in all of us.

The THRIVER is...

Fearless	**Focused**	**Expressive**	**Compassionate**
Creative	**Adventurous**	**Loving**	**Playful, Silly**
Independent	**Loves to Learn**	**Resilient**	**Connected**
Courageous	**Persistent**	**Intuitive**	
Comforting	**Fun-Loving**	**Free**	

Now go back to the THRIVER LIST you began in your journal or notebook earlier in this section. On that list, write any of these words (or others) on your THRIVER LIST.

For example, words like these might fit for you:

Integrated	**Meaningful Work**
Balanced Life	**Feel My Worthiness**
Helping, Healing Others	**Make Choices**
Connected to Inner Wisdom, Intuition, Abundance	

Now that you can feel yourself in your thriver energy, you are ready to take on the challenge of the rest of this book. As a thriver — who values things like unconditional love, family, community, helping, caring — you are ready to come up with a concrete plan and clear intentions to create the life you want and can have!

CREATING A NEW LIFE FILLED WITH POSITIVE ENERGY

I've done it, and you can too! I never dreamed that I would be writing a book like this, and yet all my life I have been a writer and have always wanted to be published. Once I got my intention deliberate and focused to write this book, here it is! I had a plan, and I put together some short- and long-term goals. What you need is a plan. In Step 7 we'll work on short-term and long-term goals that are not only focused on desires that you never imagined could actually materialize but also that come from the thriver energy inside you.

Can you feel how this is a different energy, more like what the Happy Person Inside You wrote to you in Step 3? This is a more positive, productive energy from which you can build your new life — after abuse, violence, trauma, disappointment and betrayal. Can you see how empowering this energy can be for you? And we're going to make the most of it! You are going to dream big and take risks you never thought you could. Your energy is positive, you have focused on your desires and pushed through your fears to live the life you have always wanted as a thriver.

Once you are in this energy, you are truly connected with the idea that "living well is the best revenge." Whatever happened to you in the past and whoever did it to you, what those people who hurt you didn't want was for you to live well! In their attempt to control, humiliate and destroy you, the one thing that will really get them is the thought that, without them in your life, you will do well.

Remember: Living well is your best revenge.

You are the one who is going to grow and change and prosper. Those who have abused, hurt, betrayed and disappointed you probably will not. I know this because I've worked with many women who have been abused, and I have watched their lives change forever after they began their journey to thriving. But their former partners' lives have stayed about the same. In fact, some have moved on only to find someone else they could treat as badly. Most won't make any real change for the better in their lives. That is our revenge! We are living well and they are not — it's as simple as that! So let's get on with the rest of your wonderful life!

THE EXERCISE: GETTING UNSTUCK

Do you have a sense of where you are stuck at this point? For example:

- Are you having trouble experiencing positive energy in your life?
- Do you find yourself exhausted, depressed or overwhelmed most days?
- Are your desires unclear and unfocused?
- Are you feeling lost, with no idea of what you want or could have in your life?
- What dreams have you let go of? Why?
- Are you afraid you'll never be able to push through your fears?
- What if you can't find who you really are?

Whatever step you may be stuck at (and there may be more than one step holding you back), let's write about that here before we move on. What's important about writing from the prompt below is that you don't need to be upset with yourself for getting stuck. We all do that at times. And don't feel stupid because you didn't get it until now. Your Inner Critic will jump on that and never let you shake it.

What you need is an honest, kind and loving assessment of where you are. That will help you on the road to finding the thriver in you. That's what's important — getting unstuck now.

Here is the prompt to write from in your journal or notebook. (Remember, as with all prompts, you may start in one place and end up somewhere totally different. That's okay. You can't do this wrong!)

✎ **PROMPT:** I can see that I am stuck at:

✎ **PROMPT:** To get unstuck, I am determined to start today to:

Good job! If you are stuck, don't worry. You won't be there for long. Even if you have been stuck where you are for years, you must trust that this time you will break through.

Let's try some more exercises to move into positive energy!

FUELING OUR LIVES WITH POSITIVE ENERGY

For women who are abused, sometimes the hardest thing to do is to feel good about ourselves. As we have found in previous steps in this book, often the negative energy of our Inner Critic gets us down, or we lose sight of our Happy Ending and return to a "victim" stage. There the anger and pain of our past struggles consume us and drag us down into despair, depression and hopelessness. Then too, our positive energy is low when we face problems in the present and can't see a way out of them. That's why, when a woman is in an abusive relationship or has been the victim of a violent assault, it is very hard for her to see a bright future.

In leaving that abusive relationship or dealing with a violent assault, we can begin to move out of the negative part of our lives. But it's about more than just getting out. We need to fuel our lives with positive thoughts and positive emotions in order to move beyond what has happened to us. One way is to make contact with the Happy Person Inside You as we did in Step 3. Didn't that feel good? She is a guide to our Inner Wisdom that is always positive and envisions a bright, wonderful future for us and our children.

THE EXERCISE: GETTING TO GRATITUDE!

Here's a great way to conjure up good thoughts and emotions like joy, happiness and peace that can give you momentum and propel you forward into a new, glorious part of your life.

What can be said about gaining happiness in this lifetime? I love this quote: *Happiness cannot be traveled to, owned, earned, worn or consumed. Happiness is the spiritual experience of living every minute with love, grace and gratitude.* — Denis Waitley

So if you want to fuel your journey to thriving with some of the good things in your life, you'll need to make a list! What do you love, what are you grateful for in your life right now? What are you looking forward to? What do you want to show up in your life in the future?

I call this the List of Threes — short and sweet! Don't worry if you repeat items on any of the lists on the next page. Remember: *Gratitude makes sense of our past, brings peace for today and creates a vision for tomorrow.* — Melodie Beattie

THE LIST OF THREES

✎ **PROMPT:** Make a list in threes for each of the following.

Three Things I Love:

1. _____

2. _____

3. _____

Three Things I Am Grateful for:

1. _____

2. _____

3. _____

Three Things I Am Looking Forward to:

1. _____

2. _____

3. _____

Five Years from Now, Three Things I Want in My Life:

1. _____

2. _____

3. _____

Take a look at the list you wrote from the prompts above and consider the following:

Did anything on the list surprise you? Why?

Do you repeat anything on more than one list?

What didn't appear on the list that you thought might?

Do you feel any better about what's good in your life now?

✎ **PROMPT:** Write in your journal or notebook about what surprised you or what you might have repeated as you wrote these lists. A prompt might be "I appreciate…"

All right! What you have is the beginning of what some call a "gratitude journal." Commit to writing every day — morning, noon or night, whatever works best for you — about the good things in your life. Start with the prompt — "Today I'm grateful for…" or "The best part of my day today was…" or "I love my life because…"

THE EXERCISE: CELEBRATING WHAT MAKES YOU HAPPY

Another way to bring more emotions like joy, happiness and peace into your life is to celebrate what makes you happy now or has made you happy in the past. Here's an exercise that builds on the idea expressed in this quote by Maxim Gorky: *Happiness always looks small while you hold it in your hands, but let it go, and you learn at once how big and precious it is.*

First, think about the things you do that make you happy.

For example, *I love to go to the movies. I love to go into the theater with a bag of popcorn or my favorite sweet treat and settle into my seat. When the lights go down, I feel myself go into a different world, and the problems and troubles outside the theater fade away. I feel so happy when the movie begins, and I get focused on the story unfolding before me on the screen. I love it! It makes me so happy!*

Make a list of things that make you feel that way. Jot down a few words for each item in your journal or notebook.

✎ **PROMPT:** Make a list of five things you do that make you happy.

✎ **PROMPT:** Write about how it feels to do one of them BEFORE, DURING and AFTER.

Take the time every day to enjoy something that makes you smile! What a gift! On the next few pages see what the women I have worked with have found to make them smile, too.

Smile and the world smiles back.
Change your thoughts and you change your world.
— NORMAN VINCENT PEALE

WHAT MAKES ME SMILE...

My greatest pleasure is when I am baking. I feel like I am in my own world. It makes me feel so relaxed to do something I love so much. I love to try new recipes every now and then. My biggest accomplishment is knowing that I can bake my specialty, apple pie, and it will win a ribbon. When I first entered my apple pie in a local fair, I had high hopes of winning, and yet I had grave doubts that I would. But my pie won the blue ribbon! I was so excited because this was the first time I had ever entered anything. Now that I know that I can do this, next year I plan to enter something else, and I WILL WIN! — JUDY

I have an addiction to fabric. I love it! It started when I was a teen. I took sewing lessons at the Singer store the summer when I was fourteen. A year later, I was making my own pants and wore them to high school. I used to sew during the summer when I was in college, and I wore some of the outfits I made to school. I stopped sewing for about ten years but then took it up again. Recently at a Christmas party, friends in my sewing group gave me fabric. Now the bookshelves in my family room are full of quilt fabric! — LINDA

I love being out of the inner city with time to empty my head, relax and renew. The warm sun on my skin, the cool breeze rustling through the trees, the buzzing of bees, the butterflies flitting, birds singing to each other and little old men and their remote-control sailboats. I can't wait to challenge them with my own remote control boat, but I have to practice first. Anticipation is half the fun. Sometimes I drum at the water's edge or write down my thoughts, hopes and dreams — the sound of splashing, children laughing and playing, sounds of road traffic muffled. I'm in another world, time and space, knowing I can return. — KAREN

My most favorite thing to do is to embrace the beauty of nature. I love being by the ocean, as it brings me to a place of peace within my soul. It is almost as though my wounds get washed away with each wave as they gently roll in and out. I often go to the ocean, be it winter or summer. I prefer it to be when it is less crowded so I am not distracted. There is a simplicity there. I can forget my past and not think about the future. I look at clouds and their formations and how they alter the sunlight's patterns on the waves and sand. The air is different there. The smell of the water and the sounds of the waves envelope me and cradle me to a place of peace. Oftentimes, I notice objects as I stroll along, collecting special rocks that I place in my garden at home as reminders. As a child, the water was a place that took me away from the pain, and I'd pretend I could swim away from reality to another life. — LINDA

The best thing about paddling my kayak is the feeling of autonomy she fills me with. To literally be the master of my own ship is so empowering to me. Being close to the water where there are different kinds of birds and greenery is a refreshing dose of nature. I feel euphoric for hours after my kayaking adventures. Paying for my kayak is a downer, though, so I have to hold down a job, but for me it is a positive goal and challenge. I have realized a twenty-year-old dream! — ANTOINETTE

It made me happy when I read the entire screenplay for a movie. I felt how awesome it would be to find the creativity within me to be able to write what it is I see inside my head as eloquently as other screenwriters do. While I was reading, I felt an internal energy inside, an excitement that I could envision what I was reading as if it were unfolding before my eyes. As I read each word, it was like watching the movie all over again — scene by scene. The dialogue was crystal clear as if the characters were speaking to me. After I read it, I felt an excitement to read more screenplays, but they aren't easy to come by — not just as they were written by the screenwriter. It's like a hunger for more to read in the hopes of having the process click inside my head so that I can begin to write myself. — KATHY

When it snows, I love to go sledding with my kids. Even before the sled ride, I am feeling better and more positive. I am happy with my affirmations, more relaxed. During the sled ride, I feel playful when I look at the face of my second oldest son who will soon be five years old. His scarf is full of snow from all the smashing and crashing at the bottom of the hill. He is smiling, and his face is so beautiful and crusty with snow that it makes me laugh and cry at the same time. I am looking at my youngest son sledding by himself. Drifting down the hill, so gently sliding, my baby. Afterwards, I fix hot cocoa for the boys and tea for me. My body and my mind are tired out! Ahhhhhh!! — BARB

I enjoy having a good meal with friends or my son, or both. It makes me happy to shop for the food and also to get my house looking nice. Cooking is satisfying, as is eating and having company. Simple food is best — excellent quality, not processed; everything made from scratch. I like when I can get my son to help. My preferred meal is pasta with butternut squash sauce (e.g., butternut squash, pumpkin seeds, garlic, tomatoes, salt, chili pepper, thyme, rosemary and parsley cooked in olive oil and topped with parmigiano cheese) plus a green salad and maybe some Merlot wine and, of course, water. Food is essential. — A.

Go confidently in the direction of your dreams. Live the life you imagined.

— Henry David Thoreau

Step 5
Vision a New Life

Be careful what you ask for! What I have learned in my life is that a desire for a lot of money or material things can turn into an empty wish that doesn't lead you to happiness. What your desires should take you to are the things you love and to the thriver energy inside you. Of course, you could desire abundance and enough of it so that you'd have the time and money to do many wonderful things that serve humanity!

Look at what people like Oprah and Bill and Melinda Gates, who have made billions of dollars, are doing with their money to solve some serious problems in the world. The best way to see the limitless possibilities that there are for you in the world is to visualize your future in a BIG WAY! You can do it! Do you see yourself meeting Oprah? Have you always wanted to swim with dolphins? Or do you just want you and your kids to have a happy, peaceful life?

Any and all of these dreams can come true! Being abused can make us feel hopeless and derail our dreams. But what we dream about can be ours, particularly if we focus on things that fit our values and represent our strongest passions.

To begin this process, let's continue on with our journey to thriving!

FOCUSING YOUR DESIRES

Let's review some of the wild and crazy desires that came up in your answer to the $10 million question in the survey in the Getting Started section of this book. Your list may have included things like:

SAMPLE LIST:

- Travel with my family
- Buy a house
- Pay off my bills
- Go back to school
- Start a business
- Open a center for women and children

✎ **PROMPT:** Make a list of your desires again now in your journal or notebook.

THE EXERCISE: SEEING THE FUTURE

Focusing on one or all of what you have on the above list of desires, we are going to go into the future where all your dreams have come true.

Are you ready? All right! This is going to be great fun!

You are going to write about a point in the future as if you are living it now in the present. So describe it in this way: "I'm sitting on the deck of my new vacation home overlooking the ocean on a perfect, sunny day…"

Since you are going to do this in the Happy Person frame of mind, this is your BEST CASE SCENARIO for the future! So make it big and positive!

Close your eyes for a minute, if you feel comfortable doing that, and imagine that you are moving from this space in time to the future.

Go forward into next week…

next month,

next year… three, four, five or more years ahead.

See yourself sometime in your future when all your dreams have come true! You are happy, healthy and feeling good! LIFE IS REALLY, REALLY GOOD!

Let yourself be there for a moment, noticing where you are, who is with you and how it all feels. When you are ready, open your eyes and write in your journal or notebook.

✒ **PROMPT:** Today I am living the life of my dreams. I am...

MAKE IT BIG! MAKE IT EXCITING! It's the life you have always imagined!

GOOD JOB! You are a thriver!

It must feel good to see that your future is indeed very, very bright! Make sure you put a date on this piece of writing and read it to yourself often! This a great exercise to get a visual on, too.

CREATE A VISION BOARD

A vision board is an artistic collage of images, pictures, and photos that represent your dreams and goals in a vision for the future. Creating a vision board can help you to see your goals more tangibly, and looking at your vision board daily can inspire and motivate you to achieve your dreams. Find pictures from magazines or use your own photographs to describe the future you have just envisioned. Glue them onto a large piece of paper, and when you're done, hang the collage where you can see it every day. We're going to be stepping into this vision in the next part of this book.

Before we do that, take a look at what some women I have worked with wrote for their perspective into the future! Fabulous!

Make your dreams come true — Thrive!

Whatever you can do or dream, you can begin.
Boldness has genius, power and magic in it.
Begin it now.
— GOETHE

THE THRIVER IN YOUR FUTURE

I'm sitting on my back porch in my swinging chair, enjoying the beautiful sunset, viewing the scenic garden. The sweet smell of rose fragrance fills the air. I have the luscious green grass to savor and the fresh air to breathe while I am enjoying nature and the creation of an awesome God. I am taking a quiet evening to relax from a busy day at work. Today was one of the happiest times for me. I was promoted to a manager in the company where I work, and I have a wonderful staff that loves and respects me. I really enjoy my job. After supper I take a hot bath and go to bed in the most perfect dream home that has everything I ever wanted. The air is filled with silence. It is just too perfect. It feels like no one else is around, just me and the beauty that surrounds me. Magic! What a transformation! It sure feels good. — MICHELLE

I am in my own home now. There is a peacefulness here, no intrusion and energy change like when you used to arrive. The flowers that I so carefully chose to attract hummingbirds and butterflies are doing their job. They are both dancing about, giving me the most beautiful movie. I am loved, a feeling that has been so absent in my life for so many years. It is a respectful relationship in which we are both mutually valued. My children are on their own, leading the lives that bring them happiness in their heart. I am so happy with my new job. It is both financially and emotionally satisfying. I so appreciate slowing down. I know I can sit and read or just be. I have a comfort in my soul. — LINDA

I am swimming with the dolphins. I have just completed the final level of training for my CranioSacral Therapy (CST) certification and this time is a celebration of completion of my dream to be doing the work I love. The water is warm, and my dolphin-swimming friends are all around me, sharing the dolphins' healing energy and wonderful spirit of play. This is our second trip out to swim with them, and I can feel the deep impact they are having on softening my heart and nervous system. I feel ecstatic to be in the ocean with them. I am closest to my true self here. My spirit is free and fulfilled. I was able to stay committed to myself, my work and my dreams and arrive at this day. I love my new home and partner and feel so blessed to be alive. — ANN

I'm walking on the beach at sunset in Malibu. I feel the ocean breeze wash over my face. I see miles and miles of sand and beach, and I am calm. I am content. I can smell the salt water in the air. I finally made it here, but I am not alone. I am finally free. My friends come to visit me at my beach house. I am the screenwriter I always wanted to be. I am home — where my heart needs to be, where I am finally me. — KATHY

I am sitting on the deck of my dream house, overlooking the mountains and valleys of Colorado. I have accomplished so much over this period of time in my life. I now have financial security for once in my life. I don't have to worry about where my next dollar will come from to put food on the table for my family. I have met the man of my dreams. It is so good to have someone in my life who treats me like a queen and has great respect for my son and daughter. I have opened my coffee shop, something I have always wanted to do. I was told years ago that I should go into business for myself since I was such a good baker and that I should put my talents to good use. It was tough at first, but with the hard work and determination of my children and my significant other, my business is really thriving. I have put in long hours, but there is nothing I would change. I have had the love and support of so many people through all this, and it has really paid off. — JUDY

It is a year in the future. I am very happy. I feel at peace. Life's challenges are still here, but I've learned to go with the flow, to take each day and challenge as it comes. My day care business has expanded to a real family center. My team and I care about the whole family. Sometimes it is just child care, but more often than not it is also about assisting families with financial worries, educational needs, a safe haven or networking for some needed information. I sit on my porch swing and watch the deer graze on the grass in my backyard behind my beautiful flower garden. It is early evening, and I sit here thinking of my children who are grown and come to visit often. The chain of abuse has been broken. They come with open arms and light hearts. Their relationships are happy and healthy. They have learned to give as well as take. They have beautiful babies with so much potential. The pain and struggles are so very far in the past. My life is abundant with time for work, family, play and myself. The final plans for my trip to Greece have fallen into place. I will soon be on an island surrounded by beautiful blue water. The only problem is the language which I don't know, but is not the language of love universal? And so I will survive there. — FAYE

It is June 25, 2013. We are all (my three sons and I) pitching in to put together a picnic lunch for our Saturday together. My oldest son has just given me a compliment on how incredible I am for doing such a great job on managing my last project. He is happy and well-adjusted. My second oldest son kisses me and says, "Thank you for helping me with my Cub Scout project." My youngest son wants to make sure I attend his concert next Friday night. I am happy and complete — no boogey men (fear of my ex). I am secure and happy in my house. It is our home. I have a garden, and it has tremendous color. My identity is of my own making. I am peaceful. — BARB

I have accepted fear
as part of my life,
specifically the fear of
change. But I have
gone ahead, despite the
pounding in my heart
that says, "Turn back."

– ERICA JONG

Step 6
Overcome Fears

*S*ometimes the most successful people in the world are not the most talented or the smartest. They are the ones who are most able and motivated to overcome their fears and take on huge risks to achieve their success.

Besides our fears, we also have limiting beliefs about ourselves that keep us down and form a layer of resistance that we must push through to accomplish our goals.

Remember some of those limiting beliefs from the survey you completed in the Introduction to this book?

There is no way I can create the life I want right now.
My biggest fear is that I'll never get my life together.
I'll never figure out who I am or what I want to be when I grow up.
I don't take any big risks. Life is too scary.

These are the kind of beliefs that can hold us back from manifesting our desires or even finding positive energy in our lives, both of which are important to do on the journey to thriving. Remember, on that journey we must move from:

VICTIM ⇨ **SURVIVOR** ⇨ **THRIVER**

When we are in the "victim" stage of our journey, our fears and limiting beliefs about ourselves run the show. That's harder to do when we feel more like a survivor. Yet to really manifest our dreams and thrive, we need to use the momentum of the positive energy gained in Step 5 to push us through our fears and limiting beliefs here in Step 6.

TOP TEN FEARS IN LIFE

FEAR OF...

1. ABANDONMENT — I'm afraid that someone will leave me, and I'll feel alone and vulnerable. This makes me feel unloved and unlovable.

2. REJECTION — I'm afraid that someone will tell me to go away, and I'll feel bad. This could happen in the workplace, relationships or business.

3. FAILURE — I'm afraid that I'll fail again like I have in the past.

4. SUCCESS — I'm afraid I might do something right, and the struggle will be over. What will I do then? I fear it will all be taken away from me.

5. BETRAYAL — I'm afraid someone will be unfaithful or disloyal to me. To avoid that, I let someone else define who I am or set limits on me.

6. LONELINESS — I'm afraid I'll be alone and feel lonesome. Can I learn to be alone without feeling lonely and spend quality time with myself?

7. ILLNESS — I'm afraid I'll get sick and I won't be able to do something that could make me happy or move my life forward.

8. AGING — I'm afraid I'm too old to start over, or to be taken seriously. I need to learn that I don't have to act my age or be defined by it.

9. LOSS — I have lost so much in my life. I'm afraid I'll lose more.

10. DEATH — I'm afraid that when I die I will cease to exist. Doesn't our spirit transcend death? If so, then our birth is harder than our death!

THE EXERCISE: PUSHING THROUGH OUR FEARS

What kind of fears do we have? Take a look on the previous page at the list of Top Ten Fears in Life and do the following exercise in your journal or notebook.

✐ **PROMPT:** Pick your top three fears from the list of Top Ten Fears in Life and write them in your journal or notebook.

How can we counter those fears?

✐ **PROMPT:** Write some limiting statements based on the fears you have.

EXAMPLE:

Fear of failure: *I will never get my life together.*
Fear of success: *Whatever I might accomplish, it will be taken away from me.*
Fear of loneliness: *I am incomplete without someone else.*
Fear of rejection: *I have suffered too much. I'll never get over it.*

✐ **PROMPT:** Let's respond to each of those fear-based beliefs about ourselves.

EXAMPLES OF LIMITING BELIEFS	**MY RESPONSE**
Fear of failure:	
I will never get my life together.	*My life is unfolding perfectly!*
Fear of success:	
Whatever I might accomplish,	*I celebrate my successes.*
it will be taken away from me.	*Each one has a lasting impact on my life.*
Fear of loneliness:	
I am incomplete	*I love who I am! No one else defines me.*
without someone else.	*I am unique and special.*
Fear of rejection:	
I have suffered too much.	*I am moving on with my life.*
I'll never get over it.	*I look forward to the great things ahead of me.*

Here's an ACTIVITY idea for you: Take the list of responses to your fear-based beliefs and turn them into affirmations like the ones you created earlier in this book. Write these affirmations on pieces of paper and post them about your house — on the bathroom mirror or on your computer monitor so you can see them every day and absorb them.

All right! Now that we have shifted our limited beliefs and fears into unlimited potential and positive energy, let's write about how amazing freedom from fear feels.

REMEMBER! You have no fears. Nothing is holding you back now! Go for it!

MAKE THIS BIG! Play some music before and as you write from this prompt in your journal or notebook.

✎ **PROMPT:** "If I had no fear, I would…"

When you are finished writing, read what you have written out loud. You need hear what that gutsy, fearless part of you has to say and use the energy of this moment to help push forward the future vision you have for yourself.

For further inspiration, you can also read below what some of the women I have worked with have written from this prompt.

IF I HAD NO FEAR…

…I would complete this divorce from my ex-husband and stop having conversations with him that go nowhere except to give me aggravation and guilt. I'd be independent from him emotionally. I would live on my own, in my own house that I'd be proud to finance myself. I would be more aggressive in starting my own design consulting business from my home, and I would charge what I'm worth. — HEATHER

…I would ride in a hot-air balloon, shoot the rapids in Colorado, move to Jackson Hole, Wyoming, and still have a way to stay in contact with my kids and grandkids, ride horses, be a cowgirl on a ranch as a full-time lifestyle, not allow so many self-imposed restrictions to hold me back, not worry about needing a significant other, write a book, let go of my craving for harmony between my ex and me, be confident that the future is going to be okay for me, allow my "happy character" persona to flourish, draw and paint more. — PAMELA

...I would move more freely in this physical realm of being, not bound by any past, present or future threat to my well-being. I would be more deeply rooted in my knowing and my own inner truth, living in my center. The storms of life have battered, bruised and broken me, yet my core remains hopeful that one day we will be happy, whole and have a place to belong where the wandering stops and we are home. I am choosing to live again after what seems an eternity of resignation. I had stopped fighting and allowed myself to die on so many levels. I am awake now again, fighting, seeking to move past this fuzzy place. — KAREN

...I would be on stage, an actor in a play, portraying a role, conveying an image, ideas, feelings, and sharing a story with the audience. I would make a living cuddling cats. I would really nurture myself with caresses, soothing words and hugs. I would parachute and soar through the sky and enjoy the landscape from the distance, enjoy the airscape in the moment. — ROBIN

...I would travel cross-country and interview people that I meet along the way. I find people's histories and how they formed their lives so fascinating. I would also embrace my own story in a less critical way. I would allow myself to be loved and to be deserving of such love. I would let go of the pain and look at it as if it were a distant memory. I would write a book from my heart and tell others what I'm going through and hope it would empower them. — LINDA

...I would go mountain climbing. It is something I think about often. It would be such a challenge to accomplish such a goal. If I could do that, I would have no fear of anything and could accomplish anything that life has to offer me. I love to hike. Being able to hike to the top of a mountain and finally get there would make me feel wonderful. I would stand up there and shout, "I finally did it!" — JUDY

...I would move to California. I would write every day until I found the story or stories inside that I want to tell in words. I would live the life that is my dream. And I would be happy doing it. Knowing that all things are possible, I would then help others to find their inner story, because we all have a story to tell. It's how we tell our stories that give us meaning. — KATHY

...I would be confident in a job and as a mother. I would have a career, and my children would be taken care of. I would not worry about what my ex was doing or planning. I would not worry about how my children would turn out. I would be encircled in love. I would go forward and know that I am provided for. My children would be free and could leave or stay depending on their truth — their strength, their weakness. I know I will never be alone. I will always be in the song of life — a job, fellowship I crave, life's positive flow. — BARB

SEEING POSITIVE PATTERNS IN OUR LIVES

I bet you can tell me right now all the bad habits you have and the self-destructive patterns you have engaged in, but can you identify a positive one? I'd say that you do have at least one, and yet you probably don't recognize it. If you did see it, it might give you what peak experience can always give you — the knowledge that you can push through your fears and find the thriver energy inside you. That will make you feel confident, centered and valued for what you have been able to accomplish. It can also spur you onto do the next thing that you thought you couldn't do.

Let's see if we can find a peak experience for you.

THE EXERCISE: FINDING A POSITIVE PATTERN

First, let's make a list of three powerful "peak" experiences that you have had in your life time. Jot them down quickly in your journal or notebook. You don't need a lot of details at this point. Just make the list with enough detail so you'll remember what each one is. This experience could be from any part of your life: your childhood, adolescence or adulthood. It may be learning to ride a bicycle, taking a canoe trip down the rapids at camp as a teenager, getting your driver's license, graduating from college, finding your first job, going back to school later in life or a skydiving experience. Think particularly of a time you had to push through some kind of fear to accomplish what you wanted to do.

✎ **PROMPT:** Write down in your journal or notebook three peak experiences now.

(Don't include details. Just write enough about them so you'll remember them.)

Let's take a look at your list. Which experience has the most energy for you? Which one makes you smile or feel really happy when you think about it? Which one is something you never thought you'd get through and you did? Which was the most risky for you? Which did you take the biggest chance with?

For some women who have gone through an abusive relationship or a sexual assault, surviving that experience was a peak one. Obviously, it was not a happy experience, but what we are looking for here is the journey and the exhilarating feeling of "I did it! I got through it!"

Now that you have picked out one of the experiences, let's write about it more. (You can write more about all of them eventually if you like.)

✎ **PROMPT:** Describe your experience in three parts in your journal or notebook.

What happened 1) before, 2) during and 3) after this experience?

How did you feel at each stage? For example, did you feel nervous before; anxious during, and, happy afterwards?

Add any fears you had to push through.

For example, if you went skydiving, did you have to work through your fear of heights or jumping out of a plane?

Here's what one woman I worked with wrote about her peak experience:

When I was thirteen years old, I went on a ten-day canoe trip to New Hampshire with fourteen other kids. I was very insecure around boys then but not much interested in them. I was also nervous because I never camped out before. I went without any knowledge. I was innocent of any dangers. My best friend had encouraged me to go with her on this trip, and if she could do it, then I could too.

It was a beautiful trip through the mountains with varied terrain from still, wide waters and open lakes to narrow, rough rapids. Sometimes we went down the river with the current, other times against the wind. At night, we could trust our counselors to help us set up camp, and when we were clean, we had dinner and told funny stories by campfire. It wasn't always comfortable, but I wanted to be brave and have fun.

Several times when we would shoot through some loud rapids, we would come to the calm bottom and look back up to where we came from. We were so amazed and so proud. We would laugh and yell in celebration. We all felt like we could accomplish just about anything after that! I have remembered those sensations often in the past thirty years.

From this piece above, you can see clearly that on the canoe trip, she established a "positive pattern" in her life. She had pushed through her fears riding the rapids, and if she could do that, she could do anything!

Now read through your peak experience description again. See if you can put your feelings and actions during a peak experience into three BEFORE, DURING and AFTER columns in your journal or notebook.

Here's some of the feelings and actions that you might have in your BEFORE, DURING and AFTER columns of your peak experience:

BEFORE	DURING	AFTER
Overwhelmed	Focus	Powerful
Feeling Alone	Give It My Best	Giddy
Lost, Helpless	Practice Often	Victorious
Paralyzed, Numb	Rehearse, Train	Empowered
Pressure	Inspired, Motivated	Happy, Free
Stuck	Take It Step by Step	Rewarding
Lacking Confidence	Gaining Confidence	Sure of Myself
Scared	Go with the Flow	Proud
Not Smart Enough	Learn by Doing	Experienced
Challenged	Determined	Delighted
Nervous	Encouraged by Friend	Amazed

I hope writing about your peak experiences has exhilarated you!

Now let's look at this good, positive pattern you have outlined for yourself. You overcame fear, felt good about yourself, met the challenge and had a positive result. Forget about all those times you criticized yourself about destructive patterns and bad habits! Now you have a great example of a good, positive one to follow.

This is the positive pattern we'll use in our next Step, Setting New Goals. HAVE NO FEAR! YOU CAN DO ANYTHING!

Go for the positive pattern in your life.
When we bring what is within out into the world,
miracles happen.

— HENRY DAVID THOREAU

Tell me what it is
that you plan to do
with your one, wild
and precious life?

— Mary Oliver

Step 7
Set New Goals

*A*ll right! Now it is time to set new goals for yourself that line up with your new positive, fearless thinking. "What kind of thinking is that?" you may be asking yourself. Why, it is the magical thinking of the Happy Person Inside You, the pure positive energy of the thriver who has not only survived abuse but is now also itching to get on with a new life!

So let that energy guide you, not that victim mentality where all is hopeless, nothing ever works and there is no future.

Is that possible? Here's an example of how it worked with one woman I met when she was about sixty years old. She confessed to a long-held desire to go white-water river rafting.

Now, I knew that at her age it was unlikely that white-water river rafting would ever become her new career choice, but I could tell from the way that she talked about this dream of hers that it held great energy for her. I wanted her to take advantage of this good energy to get her life moving forward again.

So I asked her to come up with the steps she would have to take — listed in reverse order — to reach her goal of going white-water rafting. That is, I had her think about the last thing she had to do to reach her goal, then the next thing before that, then before that and so on until she got to the first thing she'd do.

Here's the list she came up with:

GOAL: Go white-water river rafting

- Get into the boat
- Pay the price of admission
- Arrive at the rafting place
- Travel to the rafting place
- Call and make an appointment to go
- Do research to find a place locally that does rafting and what it costs

I asked her to add two things to this list:

1. Identify where her fears were
2. Identify what she could do immediately in that same week to begin to make her dream come true

She could easily see that it would be nothing for her to check around and research all the possible places to go rafting in her area. She could find out costs, where they were located and get a sense of what they offered as part of the trip. I could see her getting excited to do some research that very week and most likely decide where she could go to do the trip. It was mid-winter at the time, so if she wasn't planning to travel too far, she would have to do it in the spring. But that wasn't the step that held her greatest fear. Instead, she said what terrified her was getting into the boat! "No problem!" I replied. "I can be there with you as you get into the boat!"

About six months later on a Saturday in mid-May, I got a call from this woman. I could hear the excitement in her voice. She had just finished her first white-water rafting trip, and she was thrilled. She couldn't wait to do it again! And now she had a whole group of friends ready to go with her. She had done as we said — she got support to push through her fear.

Here are a few things I learned from doing this goal-setting exercise:

- Reaching a Goal Can Energize You: While many goals, like the ones you'll see below from women I have worked with, can get you to another place in your life, you also need goals that will help raise your positive energy. Find something that energizes you, and you won't stop there, I promise you!

- Reaching a Goal Can Teach You: When you push through your fears, by going white-water rafting, for example, you learn you can do ANYTHING!

- Reaching a Goal Is a Step: Reaching short-term goals can get you to long-term goals. Getting your finances in order gets you to buying a new house.

THE EXERCISE: SETTING NEW GOALS

PROMPT: Pick a goal. This isn't as hard as it seems. Look back at one of your desires from Step 5, Vision a New Life. You can also look at what you wrote earlier in this book on the survey: "If I had $10 million and all the time to do whatever I wanted to do, I'd…" Take one of those "big ideas" if you like.

Remember! *A goal is a dream with a deadline.* — Napolean Hill

PROMPT: Write down the goal and the steps. Use the worksheet on the next page and start with the *last* thing you will do to reach your goal. We are going in reverse order for a reason. We want you to feel the energy of finishing that last thing and fuel your tasks going backward from there. Sometimes it is hardest to take the first step toward a goal!

PROMPT: Where are your fears? In the steps you listed, where are your fears? Remember the list earlier in this book. Is it a fear of failure, of success, of rejection? Or is it a more physical fear, like getting into the boat to do white-water rafting? What support do you need to push through your fears?

PROMPT: What can you do in the next week? You want to get yourself moving right away and get your energy going to motivate yourself to push through your fears. It could be a simple first step, but a step in the right direction — and with it, you can begin.

> *The secret of getting ahead is getting started.*
> *The secret of getting started is breaking your complex*
> *overwhelming tasks into small manageable tasks, and then*
> *starting on the first one.*
>
> — MARK TWAIN

MY GOAL IS...

The last thing I will do to reach my goal is:

_____

_____

The thing to do before that:

_____

_____

The thing to do before that:

_____

_____

The thing to do before that:

_____

_____

The thing to do before that:

_____

_____

The thing to do before that:

_____

_____

The thing to do before that:

_____

_____

The thing to do before that:

_____

_____

The first thing I need to do:

_____

_____

What I can do this week to get started:

_____

_____

GOAL SETTING WORKS

I have been so proud of the women I have worked with who have done some amazing things as a result of this goal-setting exercise. You can, too!

As you complete your work in this section of this book, I invite you to take the survey again that was included in the Introduction. Compare your answers to see where things might have shifted for you. Even your answer to the $10 million question may have changed!

SAMPLE GOALS

Below are some of the goals that have actually been set by women I have worked with. Many of them have been accomplished. See more about some of those women and the incredible strides they have made in Meet the Thrivers!

GOAL: Get a New Job

- Arrive at my new job on first day of work
- Take kids to child care — Fear: Will they be okay? I'll miss them!
- Get in car to go to work
- Decide what to wear to first day of work
- Arrange day care for kids
- Get job offer. Negotiate salary and benefits — Fear: Did I do the right thing?
- Do job interview — Fear: I'm not good at selling myself.
- Get contacted to come in for job interview
- Send in resume for job
- Find job opening
- Assess my job skills, kind of job I want, what hours I need

This Week: Research jobs

Overcoming Fear: Plan special time with my kids on weekends

GOAL: Start a Home Interior Decorating Business

- Work with my first customer
- Make business cards, do marketing

- Set up business
- Write a business plan
- Find help with financing — Fear: No start-up money
- Start decorating houses with friends and relatives
- Take formal decorating classes

This Week: Research where classes are available

Overcoming Fear: Find someone to help me write a business plan

GOAL: Sell My Handmade Purses

- Have an opening event to display my beautiful purses!
- Create a beautiful display
- Plan date of opening
- Set up website to sell purses
- Approve web design
- Create catalog of purses
- Photograph purses I have made
- Make purses for samples
- Create design for purses

This Week: Believe in myself, my talents — Fear: I don't deserve success.

Overcoming Fear: Write affirmations about worthiness

GOAL: Open a Center for Abused and Neglected Children

- Welcome everyone to grand opening celebration for the home
- Get home ready to open
- Do renovations to home
- Purchase residence
- Get loan/mortgage to purchase home
- Get a job to finance my project
- Look for job — Fear: I haven't worked for awhile.
- Get letters of reference

This Week: Set a vision for the home.

Overcoming Fear: Do some volunteer work first to ease back into the workplace

GOAL: Open a Ranch for Abused Children to Help Them Heal with Animals

- Greet everyone at the ribbon-cutting ceremony to celebrate opening the ranch
- Construct ranch, hire staff, get animals, set up stables
- Design facility
- Purchase property
- Do fund-raising for money to buy property — Fear: I hate asking for money!
- Form a nonprofit organization, establish philosophy

This Week: Obtain support, find people who share my vision

Overcoming Fear: Find a good fund-raiser to help me

GOAL: Expand My Business Internationally

- Attend grand opening of the flagship store in another country
- Travel to that country
- Plan launch of products to sell in a foreign country
- Hire international representatives and marketing people in a foreign country
- Attend trade shows to identify products that would sell well in foreign lands
- Hire public relations people to develop campaign for products
- Raise money to develop products to sell

This Week: Research and find a business adviser who can help me with a plan

GOAL: Write My Life Story

- Have a book signing event for my family, friends, the WORLD!
- Get my book published
- Find a literary agent to represent me — Fear: My book is not good enough.
- Find editor to read and polish my book
- Write the book — Fear: I won't finish it.
- Draft outline
- Schedule time to write

- Attend writing class

This Week: Research where writing classes are held

Overcoming Fear: Join a writing group to keep motivated and on task

GOAL: Start a Custom Sewing Business

- Greet customers on my first day of business
- Find a store to sell my products — Fear: Will people pay for them?
- Produce products
- Search for and develop patterns
- Design unique products
- Go to craft fairs and other places to get ideas of what is on market now

This Week: Buy materials, do some sewing, be creative!

Overcoming Fear: Find products like mine and check out prices. They will pay!

GOAL: Move to a House in Maine

- Sit in my home overlooking the ocean
- Move to the house
- Pack up my old house
- Buy the house in Maine
- Get financing for house — Fear: Is my credit good enough?
- Pick out house
- Vision the house
- Talk to a financial planner

This Week: Research and find a financial planner who can help me with a plan

Overcoming Fear: Go on Internet to get free credit report and check my credit

GOAL: Go into Retirement

- Go to my retirement party on the last day of my job!
- Quit my job
- Contribute the maximum amount to my retirement account

- Set up budget plan to pay off my bills
- Find a source of additional income (sell my jewelry and craft items)
- Have a tag sale to liquidate things, add proceeds to retirement account
- Follow advise of financial counselor — Fear: I can't stop spending money!
- Make an appointment to see financial counselor

This Week: Research to find a financial counselor

Overcoming Fear: Find support group, ask friends for help in curbing my spending

GOAL: Expand My Day Care Business on a National Level

- Enter the national market for day care centers
- Sell myself and my model at a national conference — Fear: I've never done this!
- Articulate (e.g., write about) my model of working with children and families
- Survey, talk to my customers to find out what they like about my center

This Week: Celebrate that what I am doing is unique and helps others

Overcoming Fear: Talk with others who have made such presentations

GOAL: Make Speeches about My Story of Abuse

- Stand up at a speaking engagement and talk! — Fear: I'll cry, I'll freeze! Yikes!
- Find places interested in having speakers on this topic
- Work on a speech, outline what I want to say and what is unique about my story
- Get training as a volunteer community educator with a victim services program
- Call about volunteering for a program

This Week: Research which programs are looking for volunteers to speak

Overcoming Fear: Practice my speech with family and friends

GOAL: Travel to Hawaiian Islands

- Enjoy the first day of my great travel adventure
- Get on the plane
- Pack my suitcases
- Take time off from work

- Purchase tickets for trip
- Save money for trip
- Find a group to travel with — Fear: I hate traveling alone.
- Contact travel agent
- Decide where I want to go on the islands
- Research where to go, how much it will cost, how long I'll be gone

This Week: Get on the Internet and find information about Hawaii

Overcoming Fear: Find a great group to travel with

GOAL: Go to Art School

- Walk into my first class
- Get ready for first day of school
- Get scholarship money for school
- Register for classes
- Apply for scholarship
- Speak to counselor about classes I need and how to get money to attend
- Get admitted into school
- Go to admission office and apply to be admitted
- Visit schools I'm interested in — Fear: I don't want to go alone.
- Research schools that I could attend
- Talk to others who have attended art school

This Week and Overcoming Fear: Invite someone to go with me to visit schools

GOAL: Swim with Dolphins

- Be in the water with the dolphins
- Travel to the place — Fear: I hate to fly!
- Decide what place to go to
- Get money to do this
- Research places where you can swim with dolphins
- Write about how it will feel to swim with dolphins
- Go to aquarium to see dolphins

This Week: Find a free pass to an aquarium

Overcoming Fear: Tell myself I can fly because I want to swim with dolphins so much!

GOAL: Get My Photography Out There

- Have one of my photos in a national magazine — Fear: That I will succeed!
- Submit my portfolios
- Develop a marketing plan
- Talk to other photographers about how they do marketing
- Buy a book about marketing, learn the business side of things
- Get my photos up on the computer
- Learn more about computer and how to use software with my photos
- Organize my photos
- Take more pictures, scout out locations
- Get better digital camera

This Week: Research cameras and their prices on the Internet

Overcoming Fear: Remember the excitement of seeing my photos in print

If you want to be happy,
set a goal that commands your thoughts, liberates
your energy, and inspires your hopes.

— ANDREW CARNEGIE

There are some people
who live in a dream
world, and there are some
who face reality, and
then there are those who
turn one into the other.

– DOUGLAS H. EVERETT

Profile of a Thriver

What about the women who are thriving today after horrendous stories and lives of abuse? Who are they? How did they do it? Could you be one, too?

Remember our working definition of thriver from earlier in this book:

A thriver is a happy, self-confident and productive individual who believes she has a prosperous life ahead of her. She is on the brink of a new life, ready to follow her dreams — go back to school, find a new job, start her own business or write her story. She believes in herself and in her future so much that she will not return to an abusive relationship. She speaks knowledgeably and confidently about her experiences and is not stuck in her anger or need for revenge.

Living well is her best revenge!

You too can become one of the new breed of women who are moving on after overcoming violence and abuse. You can push through your fears, rediscover the positive energy in your life and forge a new future for yourself and your children.

After reading this book and working through the exercises in it, you will feel the thriver energy inside you. It might feel uneasy or unfamiliar to you at first, but don't let your Inner Critic tell you it's not real. It is as real as the negative energy and bad feelings you had when you were abused or assaulted. Unfortunately, your Inner Critic would prefer that you stay stuck in "Why did this happen to me?" rather than "Where can I go next?" But you can move forward with your life.

Here's how one woman described the shift she felt:

Working with Susan has totally changed my life. She started me on a journey to find the person I most want to be, and with the exercises she has presented, she is showing me how to get there.

These are the words of a thriver, a woman empowered to make changes in her life to move herself forward. No one can do this for you, however. As Oprah Winfrey has said, "The ability to triumph begins with you."

Clearly, Oprah is one of the great thrivers in the world. Born in poverty and sexually molested as a child, Oprah grew up to become a reporter, a talk show host, a movie star and in 2003, according to *Forbes* magazine, the first African American woman to reach billionaire status. As her wealth grew, so did her willingness to "give back" by providing funding and support to many causes, including AIDS, education for underserved children and ending violence against women.

But it is not only celebrities like Oprah who can reach the thriver stage. There are women all around you who you may interact with every day who could also be described as "thrivers." Many of them would not disclose in casual conversation that they have been abused or sexually assaulted, but it is estimated that nearly 12 million women in the United States will be abused by a current or former partner during their lifetime.

The women who have moved beyond the abuse in their lives have achieved incredible things. Below are the stories of some of the women I have interviewed for this book. You can read how they not only got out, but also where they are today. If these women can thrive, so can you!

From their amazing stories, we'll build a profile of a thriver at the end of this chapter that hopefully can inspire you on your own journey from victim to survivor to thriver. These women are just like you.

They are you!

You are a thriver!

THRIVER PROFILES

THRIVER PROFILE: PATRICIA

Age: In her mid-fifties at time of interview

Career goal: Become Chief Executive Officer (CEO) of nonprofit organization

Achievements: Was CEO of a nonprofit agency that works with women and children who have serious illnesses or bereavement issues. Awarded a masters' degree in social work. Mother of two daughters. Now a grandmother. Married to her second husband for twenty-seven years in a non-abusive relationship.

Advice to others: "I wish I would have known from the beginning that I was all right and I deserved better than the abuse I endured in my first marriage. Thirty years ago, if somebody had told me I'd have a master's degree and be doing the work I'm doing today, I would have told them they're crazy. It never would've occurred to me."

Previous circumstances: At sixteen, she met a seventeen-year-old boy who was very physically and emotionally abusive to her. She married him because she was afraid she couldn't live without him, but also because she was afraid that if she didn't, he would kill her. She filed for divorce several times, but each time, her husband was nice to her, and told her things would be different. After her father died unexpectedly, he was very supportive of her and then she became pregnant. To support her and the baby, he enlisted in the military and left for boot camp. When he came back, she was six months pregnant. Her body had changed so much that he didn't want anything to do with her. The abuse started again. He hit her so hard one night that she thought he had broken her jaw. She went to the emergency room to have it x-rayed, and when someone asked her if she needed some help, she realized that it was the first time she had ever thought of herself as a victim.

Moment of transformation: "After I had refused help, another incident happened and I knew I had to do something. My husband beat me up pretty badly and then passed out. I remember standing over his unconscious body with a butcher's knife in my hand. I wanted to kill him, and I knew I could. The only thing that kept me from doing it was my daughter. I didn't want her to lose both of her parents so I stopped."

Looking back now: "I never realized that I was being abused. If your self-esteem is low, and you've been raised with abuse, you don't see it when it first starts. You don't see it as anything other than the way life is. But if you're raised so that you're a stronger person with a better sense of yourself, the first time it happens to you, you're more likely to say, 'I'm out of here.' That's the way I've tried to raise my daughter."

Her life today: "What really amazes me is when other people that I think are extremely intelligent and bright think that I am too. That these people put stock in what I say and do makes me feel like a valuable and important human being. This is what I have wanted all my life and at last I have it."

THRIVER PROFILE: DOT

Age: In her mid-sixties at time of interview

Current goal: "Five years from now, I'd like to be retired, but even if I retire, I'll be doing work on domestic violence issues on a part-time or volunteer basis. I am inspired by the courage of women who have left abusive relationships and love working with them. When somebody asks me why I also work with men who are abusers, I tell them that if I can do something to change one man and save just one woman from being hurt or killed, I feel that I'm making a difference."

Previous circumstances: "I don't think the first man who abused me will ever change. He'll always be the same. He's always been like that. He is a mean, nasty person. My last husband, he might never hit a woman again, but he'll always be a womanizer. I don't think that'll ever change. What I learned is that cheating on your wife or partner is also abuse."

What was I thinking?: "Regarding going from one abusive relationship to another, it took awhile before I realized the second man was abusive, too. He said all the right things, like 'I don't know how a man could ever lay a hand on a woman,' and 'It's just not right!' But later I found out he beat his first wife. When I found out that he was cheating on me, he said if we were married he wouldn't do that. Excuses, excuses! When I left him for three or four days, I missed him. So I called him. 'I've been crazy worrying about you,' he said, and he was crying and carrying on. He came and picked me up at my girlfriend's house where I had been staying. 'Don't go!' she said. 'He's not going to change. It's going to start all over.' But I did go back even though I had suspected for a long time that he was cheating on me with other women. I thought that since he hadn't had a long-term relationship with anybody maybe this time it would be different."

Why I stayed: "I stayed in my second marriage because we owed money to my brother-in-law and I wanted to pay it off before I left. I stayed in my last marriage because we owned a company and had a lot of people working for us. I didn't want him to walk away from it and leave everyone without a job. Then too, a part of me still loved him. We had a great life with two homes and a new car every three years. I had an Audi, a Chrysler LHS, but looking back now, I'll keep my five-year-old Toyota Corolla with 152,000 miles on it. Today, I'm safe and sane. I AM sane."

Previous circumstances: "With my second husband, I didn't see myself as being abused; I just saw him as a mean person. I thought I was married to a mean person, and this is what happens when you are married to someone like that. I had to keep the house immaculate and he didn't want any interruptions when I was there."

What got me through: "The support groups I attended for victims of domestic violence are what helped me through. I went from one to the other, and when that one ended, I went right into another one. I knew I needed the support and bonding with other women to know I wasn't alone. Some of the things they said were exactly what I had been thinking. It really helped me to understand that I wasn't going crazy even though my husband had led me to believe I was. This is how a batterer acts."

Lessons learned: "I have learned to believe the women who have been abused. The more outlandish the story, the more believable it is. When they tell me something and then say, 'You're not going to believe this,' I reply, 'I probably will!' You see, I've either heard it before or I've experienced it."

My life today: "Working with women who have been abused has made me stronger. Seeing them and what they're going through, I know that I've been through that too, and I can see how far I've come. I look back now and think that this was something I had to go through. Otherwise I could never put myself in the shoes of the battered women I work with. I also like working with abusive men who are in batterer intervention programs.

What it is like working with abusive men: "What I find fascinating about working with men is how they talk about the incident that brought them into the group. They will say that both of them were drinking on the night of the assault. Both of the men who abused me said the same thing, that we were both drinking. Just to be able to speak up, confront these men and try to make them understand that no matter what, it wasn't her fault. That feels great for me. I can help them understand that what they did was not right, no matter what they think made them do it. It was still not right.

Sometimes I tell the men in the batterers' intervention group that I am a formerly abused woman. Their usual reaction is complete silence. Usually I will have been with the group for awhile, and they will have discovered that I am not a confrontational person. In fact, I'm a very quiet person, and if I do confront someone, I do it in a compassionate way. Sometimes they're shocked to hear that 'somebody as nice as you' was a victim of abuse. They can't believe that anyone would hit me because they see their wife or girlfriend as a bitch and that's why they were justified in hitting her. Somehow that makes an impression on them, that somebody as nice as me could get hit.

I also like doing the groups because some of the men, particularly the ones who are mandated to do the group by the court, don't want to be there when they first come in. They are there because they have to be or they won't see their children or get off probation. When they start the forty-week program, they say things like, 'I don't belong here. I'm not like the rest of these men. I'm different. My story is different. What I did wasn't that bad.' Then they will sit there with their arms folded over their chest, hardly saying two words and not participating in the group. But usually by the fifth or sixth week, they loosen up a bit, laugh with the guys and go out to have a cigarette with them during the break. You can see them get more relaxed as time goes by, and when they come to their final week, they'll say, 'I really didn't think I belonged in this group, but now I know I do.' They'll say that they have learned a lot and that they will leave the group with some helpful information and new tools that will make them a better person.

I think abusive men can change. But there are also some men who will abuse again. Sometimes we contact the man when he hasn't attended the group for awhile, and we'll find out that he has been arrested for domestic violence and is in jail. In other cases, a man might stop the physical battering, but not the emotional and psychological abuse, so that's what we'll work on with him in the group."

THRIVER PROFILE: CECILE

Age: In her late-fifties at time of interview

Current Occupation: Executive Director of a domestic violence program providing services to women who have been abused and their children.

Previous circumstances: "The abuse started when I was fifteen or sixteen years old and I was still in high school. I was dating Tony, a guy that my girlfriends thought was cute. I didn't think he was so cute, but my friends did and their opinion was much more important than mine. I did not come from a home where there was abuse or alcohol. When I met Tony, he drank a lot. As I got to know him, I found out that there was a history of alcoholism in his family.

Tony was abusive a few times while we were dating. I remember thinking it wasn't right that he abused me, but I didn't tell anyone, not even my friends. I thought that if we got married, everything would be fine. I truly believed that. We were married in 1966, when I was sixteen and Tony was only four years older than me. I finished high school, but I was pregnant when we got married. My first baby was born in October of the year I was married. I had my second child four years later.

For a year after we married, we lived with my parents, and then we moved to our own apartment. That's when the violence got very bad and began occurring almost daily. There was pushing, shoving, hitting, choking and kicking. He never punched me, but he probably would have if I went to the hospital after the beatings so I NEVER went to the hospital. I never told a soul. I never felt I deserved to be abused, but I didn't know how to get out of it. The abuse became my life. I lived every day in fear of my husband and how he was going to treat me. I was always on pins and needles. You would think we were the perfect family, a husband and wife and two children. Eventually, we bought our own home and lived in a Cape Cod house with a dog and two cats. We even had a picket fence. I didn't call the police when Tony abused me, because if I did, the town newspaper would do a write up on the domestic disturbances, a paragraph or two with details. I would be so embarrassed if there was an article about me and my husband in the paper in the town where I grew up and my parents were well known. That kept me from calling the police for a long time. I prayed that something would happen to change how I had to live, but I really loved my husband and thought if he would only stop drinking everything would be fine. But he only got worse."

How I learned about abuse: "In the early 1970s, I finally got the courage to attend an Al-Anon meeting. At that time, there were no domestic violence shelters available. I was young, only in my twenties, and most of the women at the Al-Anon meeting were older. No one talked about the physical abuse in their lives, only the mental abuse and impact of the drinking on the families' lives. I connected to how these women were feeling. I thought, 'Wow, they are fearful, too, never knowing what was going to happen from day to day or minute to minute.' Even when my husband wasn't home, I was always thinking, *What if he comes home, what will happen?*

I became very connected with this group. I went once a week for a long time, and eventually more and more women who were my age with small children joined us. They were like a family to me; they were my friends. We would do things outside of the meetings, and I'm still friends with some of those women today. A real bond was created because we were going through similar things. For a long time no one talked about being physically abused, and I didn't either. But one night, a woman spoke eloquently about how she had been physically abused for a long, long time by her husband who was an attorney and now sober. She was the first to speak about it, but after that we all did. These were the women who gave me the courage to call the police the next time my husband abused me."

Why I stayed: "One reason I stayed was that if I did leave and didn't have a job, I'd have to go on welfare, and I couldn't see myself doing that. But with the help of my Al-Anon group and what I was learning about alcoholism there, I could see that I had to stop reacting to him, which was the hardest thing that I've ever done. I didn't have to defend myself with all the nonsense he was accusing me of. He'd call me every name in the book, and I'd defend myself. It was idiotic. I had to learn what I could control and what I couldn't. I couldn't control his behavior, but I had some choices about mine. When I did stop reacting to him, his physical abuse stopped, which was a relief because it was so degrading. But even then he would still taunt me. He would commit other physically threatening acts like ripping up Al-Anon literature or my school books in front of me. After living this way for so long, I finally realized that going on welfare had to be better than never knowing if I was going to be whacked on the side of the head. So it made sense that I had to get out."

How I tried to get help: "The first thing I decided to do was finally call the police when Tony got physically abusive with me. I thought if I called them, the responding officers would arrest him, and he'd see how horrible it was to go to jail, and he'd stop drinking and abusing me. I called the police for the first time on Labor Day. Each year, Tony usually drank the day before Labor Day, on Labor Day, and the day after Labor Day. This particular year Tony became violent with me, so I ran down to our walk-out basement. I had figured out (now they call it 'safety planning') that I could keep money and a car key in an old coat down there in the cellar. When I got out of the house and into the car, I drove to a phone booth up the street and called the police. They told me to go back and wait outside my house, and they'd meet me there. When they got there, one of the officers went up to the front door of our house, and Tony opened it. My husband was really angry, but soon he realized that the officer had gone to high school with him. So they started talking, and the other officer said to me, 'It's Labor Day and he's had a few drinks. Why are you making a big deal out of this?' They didn't know that I had planned this for seven years, this big plan to call the police, and this was all they could offer me!

I took my children out of the house that night. They were very upset, and when we showed up at my parents' doorstep late that night, I finally told them what had been happening for years between Tony and me. I intended to go back home the next day, hoping that even though the police didn't arrest Tony (at that time, there were no other protections for victims of domestic violence, like a restraining order or a protective order issued by the judge), Tony might be afraid that I'd call the police again and stop his violence. But when I went back, he was very angry. It became clear to me that he had no fear of getting arrested by the police.

When I got the courage to call the police again and ended up on my parents' doorstep for the second time, I decided that I was going to leave Tony, and I contacted an attorney. At that time, you couldn't get exclusive use of the premises without a court hearing so I stayed with my kids at my parents' house for three months until the court date. Meanwhile, Tony stayed in our home because I was afraid to be there with him knowing he was going to get served with the divorce papers. That was pretty scary.

At the hearing, I was awarded the house so that my children could live there with me. Tony had to leave our home, and it was the first time in our marriage that we lived separately. During this time period, he was very angry at me. He'd call me constantly, swear at me and then call again. Although friends told me I could always hang up the phone when he called, I couldn't. I felt there was still an emotional connection between us, and even though he was calling and swearing at me, I thought he still cared. Today, I know that is not right, but that's how I thought about it then, that there was still some connection there."

What got me moving on: "Leaving Tony was a long, long process. Every time I told myself, 'This is it, I'm leaving,' I always did it in anger, and a day later I wasn't angry anymore, or I couldn't keep the adrenaline up and stay away. I wanted my relationship with him to last, but I finally realized that even after everything I did, he wasn't going to change or do what I wanted him to do. I needed to start my own life and not be so emotionally attached to him. I took things in small steps. I went back to school, and I had the support of my friends and my Al-Anon group. They gave me the courage to do things that were hard for me, including going on welfare for a period of time and calling the police on Tony. One of my biggest fears when I finally did make the decision to leave was that I might still go back to him. It wasn't that I was afraid to be alone. It was more that I wanted him."

Impact of the abuse on my children: "Being Catholic, I felt that when you get married, you had to stay together no matter what. I didn't think it was so bad for the children until I learned that violence in the home really does affect the kids. Tony never physically abused my children. However, during the years we were separated, he had visitation with the kids. Although it wasn't common at that time to require that the visitation be supervised by anyone, I insisted. I didn't want him taking the children out in the car with him while he was drinking. When Tony would come to the house to pick up the kids for visitation, he thought it was still his home, so he'd yell at the kids. His mood swings would go from being the jolly father and kissing them one minute to yelling at them to get out into the yard the next minute. I realize how terrified my kids were afterwards, how they were always on edge, worried he would yell at them. They were definitely afraid of him. Tony died about ten years ago. My sons were grown men by then. When I asked my eldest if he wanted to go to his dad's funeral, he said 'No, absolutely not.' My sons were both still really frightened of their father. I know they were really glad when I finally made the break from him."

How I found my work: "One day a friend of mine from Al-Anon called to tell me that they were looking for people who have been or were being abused to start a support group. Four of us, myself and three others from Al-Anon who also had been physically abused, got together and started a group. Remember, at this time in the mid-1970s there were no shelters or other services specifically for victims of domestic violence. We would provide support for the women who contacted us and tell them that we had places in people's homes they could go to if they needed shelter. I got on the list of volunteer homes to help other women. That's how the domestic violence program I work for today started. There was also a group of volunteers out of the YWCA and another group of women from a local church who were looking for a building for a shelter. At some point, the three groups merged into one, and some of the women became board members. Others, like myself, became the staff. One of the board members learned about a program where you could go to school full-time and work part-time and that person's salary would be paid for the first year. I took advantage of this opportunity and went to the community college on a full-time basis to get my Associates degree. I became the domestic violence program's first employee, and later that year, two coordinators were hired to run the program. Soon, with some federal money, they hired twenty-one people!"

The challenge of the work: "At the time we started, there were few battered women's programs in the country, and there wasn't much information about running one. So we really struggled as we met and talked. Some of the women were 'feminists' and I had no idea what that was! I met all kinds of people, including social workers, churchwomen, former battered women and things evolved.

Because of what I had gone through myself, I was highly motivated to help other women. I started working as an advocate, and I liked working in the system with the police and the courts because I knew from my own personal experience that this was an area with a lot of injustice for women. Still, I had a lot to learn. For example, I didn't know much about working in the legislative arena. But when we were lobbying to get the state laws changed to allow restraining orders and to get funding from the state to start up a shelter, I testified before the legislature, and I really liked that. I was shy. I didn't feel like I was the best public speaker, but I did it and felt really good that I was part of the process of making important changes that would improve other women's lives as well as my own."

Impact of this work on my life: "I was so young when all this happened to me. I had gone to school first to be a hairdresser, but when I went to college, I majored in social work and criminology, and I stayed with that. My life certainly would have been different if the abuse hadn't happened to me. Often I wonder what it would be like to not do this type of work, because today it is a part of me. The hard part of the work for me is that the system still responds inadequately to the needs of domestic violence victims. Those are the things I want to help change. It is harder to do this work after having been a victim. You don't get as much credibility. At times people have said that because I've been a victim, I can only see it one way, that I'm too biased or I don't understand the men's side of it. Still, I never feel that I should tell a woman who is being abused what to do, even if I have been a victim of it myself. She should know that she has options, choices she can make, and when she's ready, she'll do what she can do. Until the woman herself breaks free of the emotional attachment she feels, it's very hard for her to sever her relationship with the man. That's what she'll need to do — break the emotional tie. What helps her to do that is education and information about domestic violence. When she is feeling better about herself, she can take some baby steps which may seem so insignificant to somebody else, but they may be okay for her. For example, calling the police in a lot of situations is a big deal. But most women still don't call the police; only a minority do."

What is in my future: "I see myself retired in five years, hopefully living in Florida. Unfortunately, I can't imagine a world without domestic violence, but if that were possible, I think we'd have to start with early prevention programs in all the schools. It's important to get boys and girls at a very early age to recognize that abuse isn't right. Violence isn't the way to get what you want. Unfortunately, we have a society that condones violence in song lyrics, in the movies and on television, and it's gotten so much worse. I can't imagine that situation changing in the near future to end violence against women in the home, but I have hope that someday it will."

THRIVER PROFILE: BRENDA

Age: In her early sixties at time of interview

Previous circumstances: "In 1954, when I was eight years old, I was sexually abused by my mother's live-in boyfriend. I was afraid, but who could I tell? What would I say to them? Would I be relieved if I did tell?

When I was about ten years old, my grandfather said something to my mother, who asked me if something had happened to me. But she asked me in a way that made me think that she was angry with me. I became very fearful of telling her, and I asked her, 'What is going to happen?' She said, 'Don't worry. I'll take care of it.' But all I remember my mother doing was smearing potato salad onto the clothing of the man who abused me when they were both very drunk. Then she took more than one handful of potato salad and put it on his head, shirt and back. But I don't remember her saying that he had to leave our home or that anything different happened. I knew that I had to stay away from him."

The impact of the childhood abuse on me: "Being sexually abused as a child affected my whole worldview and caused me to engage in behaviors that were very destructive to me as well as to others. It led me into a lifestyle that I probably would not have had and behaviors that I probably would not have engaged in had it not been for this horrible, secretive burden that I was holding. I was always checking myself for 'Where am I?' 'Who is here?' 'What can I say?' 'What can't I say?' 'What shouldn't I say?' I kept certain things that went on in our home secret. I was the keeper of all this horror, and I lived with it."

How I coped: "When I was eleven years old, I met a guy who was thirteen years older than me. At that time, there was nothing sexual between us, but he would watch out for me. I dressed very much like a male since I didn't want anyone to see the vulnerability of my being female. I wore jeans, called 'dungarees' back then, and I bullied my mother into buying me a motorcycle jacket and pair of 'chukka' boots. My mother sent me to school every day in a beautifully ironed and starched skirt or dress and a nice little jacket and bows in my hair. As soon as I left the house, I'd take off the nice outfit and put on my dungarees, plaid shirt and leather jacket. I'd change my hair too and start my day.

By then I was out in the streets, hanging out and running around with an older crowd. Or I'd be walking around on my own, which at the time was unheard of. You didn't hear about street children then. I'd also go to different people's houses. Because I was well-mannered, used correct English and was extremely polite, people liked me. They would invite me into their homes to have dinner with them. My mother cooked every day and she was an excellent cook, but sometimes I would eat two or three different meals in one night. I would go to someone's house for a meal, then go home and eat what my mother had prepared. In so many ways what I was doing was so unhealthy, but nobody noticed at the time. It was unheard of then that a young child might have mental health problems or an eating disorder.

When I was on the street, I would hang out in warehouses or garages with older teens and young adults. They got me drinking beer and smoking weed, and because of that, I was in a haze a lot. I didn't want to listen to anything that my mother had to say because I couldn't trust her or her judgment, and I knew she couldn't protect me. So I looked to this group of young adults, who were primarily Caucasians, to insulate me and protect me from whatever danger there was out there.

I did very well in school and was an excellent student. But I was also very defiant, having come up North to live with my mother after attending a segregated school system in the South. I had great pride in being black. Both my mother and father, who was a Cuban, were black and they and my grandparents were descended from slaves. I've never had any shame about being a woman of African descent. But when I was fourteen, I began to experience a kind of rage, a terrible rage, and I would act out so horribly. When I went to visit my grandmother for a summer, I was sent to see a psychologist and then a psychiatrist, and I once again found myself at risk. Both a therapist and a teacher who was close to my family raped me. As I was being molested and fondled by all kinds of people, I felt totally out of control.

One day somebody said something to me that set me off. I took a piece of rawhide and wrapped it around this young man's throat. I was going to kill him. I was frightened by that kind of rage, but I didn't know what to do about it. After these outbursts, I would cry and fall into a heap. I stayed with my grandmother until I was fifteen, then I ran away to live with my older male friend and his family. By the time I was sixteen years old, my relationship with him turned to a more sexual one, and he became abusive. I knew the abuse had to stop, but I stayed with him off and on for seven years. He was never really excessively physically abusive. He might push me or slap me once in awhile or tell me that I wasn't going to do something. But to me, he was my man. We did marry at some point and when the relationship ended, the break-up between us was very violent. I had a relationship with him for another eight or ten years even after I remarried."

What I needed to do: "When I was nineteen or twenty years old, I got involved with drugs and unhealthy people. I knew what I was supposed to be doing, which was to finish high school, go to college, earn a degree, perhaps get a job and work toward an advanced degree. I knew that intellectually, but emotionally I was five years old. Sometimes I would be eight years old, but I could never go beyond twelve years of age. Emotionally I was a wreck. I was always feeling that something was wrong.

I did get involved with another man, someone I had known since I was about fifteen years old. He was a very nice guy, very loyal and not abusive. But because of my state of mind, he could not tell me anything. I could not hear him. Although I did marry him, I could not look at him as a husband, and I still had not made the break from my first husband. I was living a life that was horrible and definitely on the edge.

I had two children by my first husband, and when we separated, my kids stayed with me for awhile, but I had to send them to their father because with everything else, I couldn't deal with them. I realized that I had to focus on me. By then, I was thirty-three years old, and I knew I had to do something with my life. I decided to go back to school and planned to become a clinical psychologist who worked with children who had problems. I had been in therapy for many years at this point, and I needed to continue so I could have some closure and move forward.

As an adult, I ran away from home, leaving the young children I had with my second husband. I didn't tell anyone where I was. I wanted to be by myself and that was a good thing, but I felt a lot of pain about it. I cried and felt really guilty about leaving my children and putting such a burden on my husband and my mother to care for them. But I needed to be free and it helped me grow, be more introspective, heightening my awareness of my own body's cues. It made me say, 'I don't need drugs. In fact, I can't afford to use drugs.'"

How I learned to live with my past: "I know that everything I have gone through and experienced has been for a reason. I have no bitterness, no rage or anger, not at my mother, not at those men who sexually violated me, not at myself. I love who I am. I love who I have become. I don't know who I would have become had my life not been interrupted by this horrific violence and by my getting into unhealthy relationships. I recognized at some point that I really couldn't live with someone. I can't sustain a relationship because I still struggle with my ability to trust. Who do we trust and how much? What do you trust them with?"

A defining moment: "All the things that should have made me angry and bitter and caused me to have a jaded sense of my own well-being are gone! They have been lifted from me, and that shift came about in a very subtle way. I remained angry for many, many years. But when I was in my late forties and early fifties, I asked myself, 'Why am I wasting this energy? Why am I holding this stuff? Is this helping me in any way? What am I taking away from my life because I'm stuck back in another time?' I can't go back and change it. I can only go forward from where I am. I can't look for anyone to validate me or approve of me, but I can validate and approve of myself. I don't need anyone else's permission; I give myself permission.

My mother died in 2000, and I miss her every day — even with the many problems we had through the years and my mother's feelings toward me and my feelings towards her. But before my mother died, we talked about everything, laid it all out on the table. I believe it was well with both of us when she died. I had no regrets, but I wasn't ready to lose my mother. She seemed perfectly healthy the day before, and she went in her sleep peacefully without illness, without struggle, without pain. I thank God for that."

What has worked for me: "I practiced Buddhism for about eighteen years. The practice of Buddhism helped me to be able to let go of a lot of things. It brought out the best in me and taught me to be a humanist. It allowed me to see another way of life, a way of living every day and looking at life through the prism of humanism in which everything is connected to everything else. Before being a Buddhist, I had also been a Muslim and Pentecostal, although I was raised as a Christian. Today, I have gone back to my Christian faith, and it has made me feel free. Little by little, I stopped my daily Buddhist practice, and now I practice a combination — or a culmination — of all of it. I'm very content with my spirituality."

Finding my work: "At one point in my life, I realized there was something I had been wanting to do all my life, but I always stepped back from it because it got too hard. So I went to the women's center in the city where I was living and enrolled in training to work on their rape crisis hotline. At first I thought 'What am I doing? I don't know anything about this stuff!' Then a woman I met told me that I was pretty good at talking to people about violence against them. I told her it seemed to come naturally. Then one night she called me from the hospital and said, 'I have somebody who needs someone to talk to. Do you want to come over here?' I said, 'Sure.' From then, I worked at a hospital doing rape crisis counseling. It was a job, and I felt great!"

My work today: "I am retired from working in a police department as an advocate where I saw both victims and perpetrators. There, I was an activist on behalf of women, children and families. I spoke truth to power. I also dealt with issues of race, class and culture and how they impacted our ability to achieve justice and equality. As part of my job, I witnessed children in incredible pain who had been violated and had seen unspeakable violence in their homes and their environments. I saw women who were addicted and caught up in the life and thought that was okay. From that experience, I know what it is like to be caught up in all those places and to feel the great satisfaction of helping someone make sense of what they were feeling when they have been traumatized. I had come to a place in that work where I was very comfortable with it. It was like another sister, a good friend. It was like an old shoe, but every now and then that shoe would hurt. Even though I've had that shoe on for a long time and it still might pinch, that's what kept me sharp and focused. I don't know everything and I never will, but I will always see myself as a teacher and a learner. In my retirement, I do consulting with not-for-profit organizations and with my faith community, the United Methodist Women, as a member of the human trafficking team. In that work, I travel throughout the region where I live to raise awareness on the issues of domestic violence, human trafficking and immigration. To me, this work is a continuation of my earlier efforts to combat violence against women, children and in families. I know that I will always need to do work that makes a difference in people's lives. I want to do the best I can while I'm here on this earth and I don't know how long that will be."

What I have learned in my life: "I am a valuable, worthy person, no matter what has happened to me. True, I had a horrific case of arrested development. Emotionally, I was a child for a very long time because of the trauma that I experienced when I was young. But once I recognized my value, my worthiness and realized that I had goals and aspirations, I could do anything I wanted to do with my life. It is never too late. I could never be too ashamed, too embarrassed or too proud to give up and not try. I can't worry about what others think of me anymore. It is about me, and I am worth it. I'm worth putting the effort into me. Maybe no other person on the face of the earth loves me, cares about me, or believes in me, but I believe in me. I love me. I cherish my life. I am a beautiful person inside and out, no matter what anyone else may think. I love Brenda! I love Brenda. She is a wonderful woman. She is a valuable and worthy sister, and I've got to love her."

How I feel about myself today: "I came out on the other side of what I've faced in my life, and I'm no longer looking for someone to rescue me. Sure, at times it might feel better if they did, but I know that is not going to happen. Women are their own best rescuers. It has to come from inside. At some point, we have to say, 'You know what? I have to be the one to make a change.' If someone else puts the change in place for us, it does not hold or stick. It must come from within us, from our values and beliefs that we can be different if we really, really try. Otherwise, it's not going to happen."

My advice to other women: "We can have what we want. We don't have to live vicariously through someone else. Whatever you are told or taught, you must think critically about who you are and what you want from your life. Don't let someone else define you or tell you what you should be or how you should be. Be who you are and don't be afraid of that. No matter how ugly some of the pieces are, no matter how dark some of the corners may be, they are all what make us who we are."

THRIVER PROFILE: SAMANTHA

Age: In her late-fortiess at time of interview

Previous circumstances: "It was at a very early age — maybe three or four years old — that I first realized I was being abused by my father. I prayed for the day that I could leave that environment. I saw my brothers leave home when they were relatively young and I was fifteen or sixteen years old. So I was waiting for my chance. Every time I was abused, I got stronger because I accepted it less and less. But throughout my adult life, I've been in relationships that were abusive. No, I wasn't beaten or bloodied in all of them, but I was treated with less respect than what I deserved.

When I was sixteen years old, I remember my father coming at me down the hallway of our home, and for the first time, I turned around and faced him. I was willing to die rather than accept being beaten by him again. It shocked him that I stood my ground with him, and that I, or anyone, had the nerve to do that. He didn't beat me that time, but I left home shortly afterwards. I was seventeen years old and had saved $1,000 so I could pack up my car and move out of state to where my brother lived. Since my family was wealthy, I'd been raised with no concept of what things cost or having to pay for anything. My dad was very controlling and took care of everything. I didn't know what a checkbook was. He never taught us how to live independently, and we were isolated from other people. I didn't have many friends and weren't even allowed to associate with each other. We couldn't talk in somebody's bedroom alone. So I had no sense of how to function together as a family or be independent.

After I left my parents' house, I tried to put myself through school and had to work at all kinds of odd jobs to keep myself going, but it was very difficult. A short time later, I met and married somebody who was very similar to my father — very conservative, very controlling and very rigid. He was a professor at my college and older than I was. I never really dated him, but we were married within nine months of meeting each other. Suddenly I was back in a similar situation. His means of control was that we did not have sex before marriage, and we only had sex twice within the marriage, the first night and a week later. Soon after we were married, I got pregnant, and my husband convinced me to have the baby. I can see now that it was his way to keep me down and control me. I was horribly sick for nine months, vomiting every twenty minutes, hospitalized for dehydration and unable to continue with school. It was the worst year of my life, and I was only twenty years old. After being pushed down the stairs by my husband, I decided to get out of this situation because I not only needed to protect and take of myself, but now I also had a small baby. She was a blessing to me because I don't think I had enough self-esteem or self-worth to look out for what was best for me, but I could do that for my daughter. I could fight like hell and would die for her, so she really motivated me to do better.

I left that state and came back home. I got three minimum wage jobs because that was all I was qualified for and rented a one-bedroom apartment for my daughter and me. I made our life as healthy and happy as I could. Given how I grew up, I knew that you didn't have to have big houses and money to thrive. Day by day, inch by inch, situation through situation, I crawled myself out of this thing. It took years and additional abuse from my ex-husband. He kidnapped my daughter once, and he tried in every way to complicate my life. I got nothing from him through the divorce except my freedom and joint custody of my daughter."

My early goals: "I was always a bright student. I graduated high school early at sixteen years of age and I wanted to go to college. I planned eventually to go to law school. I applied to Vassar, Yale and all those prestigious private colleges. I was so proud when I got letters back from the schools that I was accepted, and I showed them to my father. I saw going to one of those colleges as my ticket out of my parents' house and a way to become a financial success and provide myself with a better life than I had growing up with my family. But my father said that he saw no reason for me to get a college education because I was probably just going to get married and have five children. Why put me through any of these top schools? I went to the financial aid office at Yale University and tried to get help, but my father was wealthy and I had to use his income since I was still sixteen. So I went to a state university near my parents' house instead. It was a good school, but after I had dreamt my whole life of going to a top school and had applied myself to my schooling, that school didn't cut it for me."

Going to college was important to me: "I still feel today that my father stole my education from me, but that didn't stop me from getting my college degree. After attending the state university for two semesters and then another college for awhile, I left school after I married my husband and had my daughter. I was not able to go back until I was thirty years old and my daughter was nine or ten years old. We had moved back to my home state, and I was working full-time during the day and going to school at night. After work, I'd pick my daughter up, put her in the car and drive for forty minutes to my class. My daughter went to school like that with me until she was fourteen years of age and old enough to stay home alone. For many years my daughter and I would sit in the back of the classroom and she'd do her homework. Later, when my daughter was older and she could sit out in the hallway, I advanced to a seat in the front of the class. By the end of my college career, I was front and center. I pursued a Bachelors of General Studies program because I wanted a well-rounded education, and I believe I got that. I loved being in school. Going to school gave me self-esteem. I was always at the top of the class, always the overachiever. I was able to support myself and my daughter with a variety of jobs, but I'm still paying off my student loans at age forty-three."

My inspiration: "Of all the people in my life, my daughter has been my greatest inspiration and the greatest blessing I could've ever had. My daughter got me through school by keeping me going every day. There were many times when I would come home and collapse on the floor and tell myself, 'I can't do this, I can't work full-time and go to school every night.' There were times that we'd have to eat pasta for the week because I could get that at five packages for a dollar. But she recognized how important it was to me. She'd said, 'You have to do this. It's not even a choice. We'll eat pasta for a week.' She was sixteen when I graduated. To this day, she has the picture taken at my graduation on her refrigerator."

Raising my daughter to be strong: "I decided that I was not going to have my daughter suffer the same fate that I had. She was never spanked, and there was never any physical or mental abuse. She was always a spunky little girl, because I always allowed her to have a voice. Now that she's twenty-two, I think I've done fairly well. She's a very self-empowered young woman. She's very much an individual, but she has had me behind her. She does realize that. Unlike her, I didn't have anyone to say, 'Yeah! Go for it!' or 'Yeah, give it a try!' She has me as her biggest cheerleader. We don't have family. It's just the two of us."

My greatest achievement: "It felt incredible to graduate from college. It took me five years to do it, but when I got my degree at the graduation ceremony, I held it up in the middle of the auditorium with my daughter in the stands and said, 'WE DID IT!' She was so elated because she knew how hard I'd worked. I'm really impressed with what I've been able to do as a single woman. I never would have thought I could do it, since I certainly was raised that no woman could ever do this."

How I found my work: "When I went back to school at age thirty, I started attending women's support groups at several local domestic violence programs. Eventually I began facilitating the support groups and doing advocacy work with women. Soon my focus changed to social work rather than law. I felt there was more freedom in doing what I could do for those I wanted to work with. I never wanted a woman to suffer the fate that I did with my parents and ex-husband, and I wanted to help women so they could leave the abuse. I didn't want any woman to reach out, only for someone not to be there to help her. I was going to be there. Once I was in a hotel elevator and a guy was going off on his girlfriend. As I left the elevator, I slipped the woman my card and told her, 'If you need to talk, call me.' She ended up coming to the support group.

After I graduated, I started a business working with women as I had in the domestic violence programs, providing counseling and support groups. I expanded to support groups, did parenting and child development classes for men and women and helped people through transitions with life coaching. Later, I learned about mediation and worked with couples so there could be kinder, gentler divorces. Mediation allows couples to separate and still keep the family intact and benefit the children. I was a real advocate for that because of the home that I was raised in.

I've been doing this work for about thirteen years, and now I focus on high conflict divorces. I work mostly with women, but one-third of my clients are men. I work with men to educate them about child development issues and help them see the impact of their behaviors on the lives of their families and ex-wives. My goal is that these fathers will be actively involved in their children's lives and learn from them. I don't advertise, except by word-of-mouth with clients, attorneys and psychologists who know me and have worked with me. I'll do whatever needs to be done for my clients. If a woman has small children or doesn't have money for child care, I'll meet them at a park. We'll go over court papers and briefs and all that while they are changing diapers. I will escort them to court, go over their testimony and make them comfortable so that their side of the story can be fully told and they won't be intimidated."

What my work means to me: "I get phone calls from clients I worked with years ago who say thank you and tell me that I saved their lives. One client told me, 'I would never have a relationship with my son if it weren't for you.' I know I've done really meaningful work. I don't know anybody else who does it. It's very unique. Each and every one of my clients has inspired me. The women have incredible stories, and the success in their lives is phenomenal. They may not be successful in the ordinary use of the word, but they have been greatly successful in what they have endured and overcome and continue to struggle with. Their lives are so full, it amazes me."

Where I am today: "Today at forty-three, I still think, 'Gosh, I did it.' It still amazes me, yet I don't think I really did it myself. There must have been a man somewhere, but there wasn't. No Prince Charming — I was my own Prince Charming. In my daughter's wedding album, she has a picture of me as both father and mother of the bride. We have always celebrated Father's Day for me. Some days it seems hard to believe that I could possibly have survived as a woman on my own and thrived without a man somewhere because I was raised from such a young age that I could never do that."

A defining moment in my life: "Before I turned thirty, I was driving with my boyfriend in his red sports car. We passed a building that was unfamiliar to me, so I asked him, 'What's that?' He said it was the university's law school, and my ears just perked up. But I didn't have enough self-esteem to believe that I could go back to school. Outwardly I appeared to have it all together, but inside I was a mess. It was all a façade. So I thought: Here I am in this sports car with this gorgeous guy, I'm wearing a size six dress and working out regularly at the gym. What I really wanted was to get rid of the boyfriend and the sports car, gain some weight, be more human and get back to school! So that's what I did!"

Dealing with the abuse: "Somewhere in me, I still want to be eight years old with my dad. He used to take me to Broadway shows and we did all this kind of stuff. He was an extremely abusive man, but there was another side of him that was larger than life. People don't understand the long-term effects abuse has on children. Adult children can make it through, but we don't hear about these stories. My dad has passed away now, and it has been deeply painful yet liberating. Ever since I was a little girl, I knew that it would take his death for me to feel truly free. I remember the good times, as he was a magnificent man in many ways. These men always have endearing qualities, or we would not be so drawn to them. On his deathbed, he told my brother to tell me that he loved me and that he was so sorry. There is a quiet understanding between my father and myself and, finally, a forgiveness (not a 'forget-ness'). I miss him. I missed him more when he was alive and there was no resolution to our issues. That hurt. Now, there is nothing I can do about that, but it is liberating."

What's in my future: "If I had a million dollars, I would sell really wild and crazy hats on a beach somewhere! I would travel, although I realize that when you go to other parts of the country there's still Wal-Mart and Kmart. I do have a thirst for knowledge, so I may go back for my MBA or a master's in social work (MSW)."

THRIVER PROFILE: CYNTHIA

Age: In her late twenties at time of interview

Current Occupation: After serving in the Peace Corps for two years following graduation from college, Cynthia now works giving programmatic support to projects involving women's and children's health in other countries.

Previous Circumstances: "At the end of my sophomore year at college, when I was nineteen, I was assaulted by a friend — not a great friend, but a friend that I trusted and never would have considered that he could do anything to harm me. He knocked on the door to my dorm room late at night and told me that he had been locked out of his bedroom and needed a place for the night. He asked me if he could stay with me and since my roommate was out of town that weekend, I said that he could sleep in my bed and I'd sleep in hers.

After we both lay down, he got up and left the room. I thought he had gone to the bathroom, but when he came back, he came to my bed, got on top of me and held me down. I didn't scream because I didn't want to make him more angry and maybe hit me, so I kept quiet for awhile. Then I said, 'No, no, no. You need to stop. Can you please stop?' He did stop for awhile and lay down next to me. I thought I'd wait until he fell asleep and then run out the door. But he got on top of me again and put his hand on my hair so that I couldn't move my head, and he held my wrists. He was touching me, and I thought he was going to rape me. I didn't know what to do. The week before we had had self-defense training on campus and I remembered the trainer saying that he'd have to lift himself up to take my clothes off and get inside me, so I waited until then, and in that moment, I got off the bed and ran out of the room. I went into the bathroom and stayed there for a few minutes. Then, without going back into the room, I went to see if he was still there, and I saw him going out the window."

The way I chose to deal with the assault: "I had always thought that the first thing I'd do in a case like this would be to call the police, but I didn't. I went into my best friend's room and told her what had happened. We called campus security, and by four o'clock in the morning others on campus had been notified. When I was waiting for campus security to come talk to me, I called my parents. That was the hardest thing for me to do. I didn't know where to start, so I said to my mom, 'I have something to tell you. I have been sexually assaulted by a friend.' Of course, she wanted to come right away, but I said, 'No, it's okay. I'm fine. People are taking care of me.' I had to hang up because someone had come to talk to me, so she said, 'I'll call you back.' When she phoned me about fifteen minutes later, she said, 'I don't care if you don't want me to come or not. I'm coming because you need one of us to be there, and I'm not sure that your dad should come.'

My mom arrived about two hours later. By then, I had finished talking to everyone, and my best friend was making sure that everything was being taken care of. We had asked one of the people from the college if we should call the police. They said I could do that if I wanted to but that I didn't need to. They explained that there was little evidence of what had happened, and going to the police would start a long process that I'd have to wait for to conclude. I was going on study abroad in three months so if it took longer than that, I might have to fly back, and I wasn't sure I wanted to do that. They explained one of the options I had within college called the 'jurisdiction process' and how it worked. They said it could be done before the end of the school year. After considering all of that information, I thought the jurisdiction process was the best thing to do. Before it started, he was moved to a different dorm building. I wasn't allowed to talk about the events and the name of the person involved. They convened a three-person jury panel (two faculty members and one student) that we met with, and I had the option of not being in the same room with the attacker during the process. Since I didn't want to see him at that point, I chose that. We both read our statements about what had happened and how it made us feel. He admitted to what he did, but he said he never wanted to hurt me. I don't know that I believed him, but he still didn't see what he had done as being very traumatic to me. Because he hadn't physically hurt me, it wasn't considered so bad. However, he cried when I explained to the panel how what he had done had changed my life."

How the process was resolved: "I suggested several different outcomes for him in the jurisdiction process. First, I wanted him expelled from school, but if he was allowed to stay, I wanted him to write a statement about what he did and how it had had an impact on me. I also wanted him to take a women's studies course. As for his list of outcomes, he didn't want to leave the school or have any limitations on him. In the end, he was suspended for one semester and in order to come back, he had to go to counseling and take a women's studies class. He wasn't allowed to go on study abroad and when he returned to school, he couldn't take part in any senior events except graduation or be on school premises except for school-related activities or classes.

When I returned to school after studying abroad in my junior year, we only ran into each other a couple of times, but it was harder in our senior year. During fall quarter we were in a class together. When I went to ask about it, I found out that it wasn't one of the limitations that he had. It felt too uncomfortable for me to sit there every day with him, but the class was in my major and his minor so I asked through the Dean if he would leave the class voluntarily. But he wouldn't, and I found out that I had enough credits in my major to graduate, so I took another class. He was ostracized on campus for what he did to me, but only by students who knew me better. There were some people who had asked him why he hadn't been there for one semester, and he told them he had been suspended due to a sexual assault. Most of them didn't think too much about it."

How the assault impacted my life: "I was standoffish toward all men following the assault except one of my very good male friends. Ultimately, I severed quite a few friendships with both males and females because I didn't feel that they were supportive of me. A woman friend took the view, 'Why did you let him into the house that night? You didn't know him very well.' But she wasn't there, I was. There were also some men that I dropped as friends, but they were the ones that I already disagreed with on certain topics. I hung out with people who thought like me on women's issues and most other topics. When I went to Japan to study abroad, even though I was in a different culture, there were a lot of American men from other colleges on that trip who didn't seem to have a good view of women, so I hardly ever hung out with them. It was one of my other male friends who brought me out of the cocoon and reassured me that not all men were bad. But even with my female friends, a lot of people want to blame the woman for being sexually assaulted. They think it's not about power and control but sexual desire. In my case, it didn't matter that I opened the door to him, it didn't give him the right to hurt me. I still pick and choose who I tell that I was sexually assaulted. I don't think that everyone needs to know, but I do tell people who have known me for awhile if I think it will strengthen our friendship. It's part of my experience. To understand me, they need to know that it did happen to me."

A defining moment for me: "The day I graduated from college was hard for me. I hadn't expected the man who attacked me to be at the graduation ceremony, and I didn't want him there. So I wrote him a letter through one of the deans, explaining how graduation was supposed to be a day of rejoicing and celebration and it would be very hard and unfair to me to see him applauded in front of everyone. But he told the dean that he was going to go to graduation and I couldn't do anything about it. The night before the ceremony, my friends got together and made stickers saying "Stop Violence against Women" that we handed out at graduation. An amazing number of people put them on, mostly students I knew, but one professor did too, and that was very cool. I had a lot of support that day from family and friends. It helped me take my power back, and I realized how important it was for me to let my story out there and have people understand how it impacted me (and impacts society as a whole.) Now I can see how dominance and power works and how people can very easily oppress others, especially when they don't have the social networks and support systems I had to help me."

My advice to women: "I would tell a woman who has been sexually assaulted, 'Listen to your emotions. Afterwards you'll go through a lot of different ones, like being sad and depressed one day, then the next day being really happy and then the following day, you are really angry. People will say you shouldn't be so emotional, that you need to get over it or forget about the assault. But you can't forget it. You have to incorporate the experience into who and what you are and go through all the emotions in order to heal. It took me awhile to get angry and when I got there, I was really angry at him, but also at the people who couldn't understand the situation I was in, that it wasn't my fault. The anger came in spurts and it stayed that way for about a year. After the anger stage, I went to a more calm, patient and happy place. What's most important is to ask for help and get the support you need. It's amazing how little you know about your support group until something really bad happens, and how much they can be there for you if you ask for help.'"

How I moved on: "About two years after the assault, I went back to stay in Japan for a few months, and being in a different place did help me. It felt like a chapter of my life had closed, not totally — but to some degree it was behind me, and I could move on. Not having to see him again had something to do with it, I am sure. I do still wonder where he is and what he is doing. Not because I want to wish him luck, but more because I want to make sure he hasn't hurt someone else. I feel like I have closure. I'm not a very forgiving person. I'm still thinking that there are some things you can never forgive someone for. I don't feel bad about that. Some people say that I should forgive him. Somebody said that I must have forgiven him to some extent, because I talk to men and have moved on with my life. I don't know if that is forgiveness, but I definitely feel like it is closure. But like any other experience in life, it changes things, and even negative experiences can make you who you are. I won't ever forget it and don't necessarily want to, but even though I don't revisit the negative feelings as much now, I'm still not at the end of my journey."

The reason for my success: "I attribute my success to the support of the wonderful feminist women in my life who were always there for me and appropriately angry toward him. Also, my male friends were great. When I explained things to them, they knew the right things to say, like 'I'm glad you feel comfortable enough to share that with me,' rather than, 'Why are you telling me this?' I often wonder what it would have been like if those supportive friends had not been there for me. If the majority of the people around me would have been like the person who said 'Why did you open the door? You didn't know him that well,' maybe I wouldn't have come out of this so strong. I also have to credit my parents for supporting me. I have friends who have been sexually assaulted and chosen not to tell their parents. Everyone has to decide that for themselves, but I couldn't imagine not telling them, although it was extremely hard to do. They have been very understanding. My dad was great when I got angry after the assault and said that I hated all men! My mom and dad were my biggest strengths and it was great that my mom knew that day even when I said I was fine, that it was important for her to come and be with me. She helped me to relax and get through the day and do what I needed to do. I'm still working through some trust issues today regarding being in a relationship or interacting with men. I'm hoping that in the future I'll learn to trust new people 100 percent rather than just 98 percent. But I am strong now, and I will continue to be strong. I was strong when I was assaulted too. I know now that overall I am the person who won here, not the person who assaulted me! All this has been part of my process of understanding my feminist background. Although my mom and grandmother aren't comfortable calling themselves feminists, I realize now that I got my feminism from them. I also know that this process of finding myself as a woman had already begun before the assault, but because of it, maybe the process went more quickly than it would have otherwise."

My future: "I want to work with women and help them have a voice. I want to have institutions and programs developed that are more about what women need than what others think they should want. While I was in the Peace Corps, I learned about the positive ways that women face obstacles in their lives and the most effective ways to give people new information. I am currently working in the United States and learning more about the donor system. By having field and programmatic experience, I am hoping to start my own organization in the future."

THE EXERCISE: FEELING THE THRIVER ENERGY

Aren't these stories inspiring? I love to read them. It is clear what made these women not only survive but also thrive. Write down in your journal or notebook what things these women did in order to succeed on their journey. I've put my list below for you to consider too.

✎ **PROMPT:** Make a list of things that helped these women thrive.

Here's my list:

1. Identified themselves as victims, got services they needed
2. Survived their abuse
3. Followed their dreams
4. Took care of their kids, planned for their futures
5. Gave back to their communities, helped other women get out
6. Showed strength and courage
7. Pushed through their fears
8. Found support in other women who have survived and thrived
9. Built their self esteem and self worth
10. Never looked back, never gave up, moved on!

Take a look at your list and mine and see what that journey to thriver requires of you. To get even more inspired, take a look at the testimonials on the next few pages that were written by some of women I have worked with over the last fifteen years. Read how each woman came to her own sense of well-being — that things were going to be all right — and how she found a community of women and friends who truly loved and supported her.

One woman describes her journey to come to America; a second one to leave the person who abused her as something that always reminds her that feeling free is the core of her thriver energy. Another woman writes a letter to her mother frequently, telling her how much she misses her since she died and how her loving, caring spirit lives on for her. Still another woman used the fairy-tale exercise (See Step 1 of this book) to remind herself how she can look within to find her beauty, her thriver energy and the assurance that all will be well. Additional thriver stories in the next chapter will inspire and delight you even more.

There is a lot of positive energy out there. All you have to do is tap into it!

TESTIMONIALS ON FEELING THE THRIVER ENERGY

I believe that the first time I reached a moment when I felt I was going to be okay was when I moved into my own apartment and began living by myself. I found that so many of my imagined fears and the beliefs that I had about loneliness and unhappiness were not there. Actually, I was more lonely, isolated and unhappy in my marriage with so many distractions around me. Now that I have left the marriage and live on my own, I experience joy and peace in my everyday living. I really surprised myself and am proud that I did it. — VIRGINIA

I had a feeling of peace when I called the lawyer to go forward with my divorce. I had such a feeling of freedom that I asked both my lawyer and counselor why I was feeling so good, having no fear or sadness. They told me that I had walked into my own power. It is true that I have taken my life into my own hands and am now making my own choices. It is bringing out the best part of me, and I'm finding out the real truths about my life. My greatest prayer is that I may be able to learn to love myself, to treat myself with kindness and respect. I love the person I am becoming, not the person that I was. I love finding my own individuality. It is not wrong to be different. I had a breakthrough when I could see why I felt different from others. I believed the lie, that if I showed how I was different than others, I was wrong and bad. There is great joy in realizing that it is okay to be different, to be me. — ADRIENNE

I am doing things for myself now and slowly making friends with positive, supportive people who like me and tell me, 'Darlene, you are a beautiful person!' As I go out and try things, God and the Universe are helping me. I put it out there and see what happens. I don't even ask sometimes, and still it is waiting for me. I now have responsible, friendly people around me who truly care about me. I found this to be true when I went to my salsa, merengue and bachata dance classes. Boom! I found two new friends there! Then I was afraid to go out in public and practice my new dance moves. But I was invited to a birthday happy hour by some coworkers and we went to a place where you could dance, and I felt safe there. I met two new friends! Now I'm doing zumba classes and it is crazy — I'm shaking things I've never shaken before, and I want to shake some more! I feel sexy! I believe that all this dancing has helped me become more confident in myself. I love the music and the movement. The exercise is great fun! I want to be the most sexy senior in town. I can dance all night and still wake up the next day without feeling sore. I am making friends who love, support and encourage me. It is exercise with a spiritual flair. — DARLENE

Twenty-one years ago — oh my God! Already so much time has passed — I was so happy. I was jumping up and down and singing for joy. I was free finally. My dream had come true. It was the time I broke away from my country where I felt I wasn't welcomed because I wasn't one of "them." I couldn't embrace the politics of my country. It was the time I broke away from my family, but I wasn't sad. I felt I needed to take off without anyone's permission. Later, I got to a new land — the land of my dreams. I always thought that it would make me the happiest person ever. In the United States, I met new people, including the father of my son. For many years, I couldn't see the reality, I couldn't see the abuse. I thought it was normal for him to be that way, but then one day, after being together for sixteen years, I broke away again. I broke away from the person who made me suffer. I had a job, and I had my son. I had to do something for my son, for his future and my life. I found the power to break the spell and move again away from the abuse, just my son and me. I was getting more powerful day by day. I found a place that I call my sanctuary. It's my home. I'm safe. I can make decisions for my son and me. It is peaceful here, and I found joy when I joined the workshops that Susan conducts. Today it is wonderful living my life. It is full of abundance, knowing all these wonderful women whose lives weren't easy because there was someone trying to break their hearts and souls too. But now, like me, they are free, and I am content and very happy to be with them. — ANNA

Dear Mom, I still miss you when I see all the butterflies flying around outside. I went to the camp with Dad and my new stepmother last week. I saw all the butterflies flying there too, and I thought of you. I swam in the water, and I picked up handfuls of white stones to put on your gravestone. I know that you like moonstones, so I guess it was good to pick up white stones and shells. We are here again at the My Avenging Angel weekend retreat for the fourth year in a row. I picked up more stones this year, and I decorated my journal with hearts and butterflies. Now I feel the peace coming into my life. Soon I will be in someone's wedding party, walking down the aisle with some guy that I don't know. I will meet him on that day of the wedding. We will see if he likes me. I still listen to your favorite songs. — LOVE, YOUR DAUGHTER, KARLA

The wound is the place
where the light enters you.

— RUMI

Surviving is important.

Thriving is elegant.

— Maya Angelou

Meet the Thrivers!

This is a very special chapter for me. In it, I'm going to share with you some of the great success stories of my life. You will be meeting some of the brave and amazing women that I have worked with since I started helping women take the journey from victim to survivor to thriver in 2001.

In a variety of ways, these women found me and the work I was doing at the time with the My Avenging Angel Workshops™. They came not knowing what I had to offer, what they'd find there, but they had this crazy idea that maybe, just maybe, they could move beyond the abuse in their lives.

And they did it. Now they and the hundreds of other women I have worked with are a special part of my life. Several of these women regularly accompany me when I speak or do trainings about my work. Often it is hard for me to explain to the audience exactly how the transformation from survivor to thriver happens and what it feels like. So these women — my thriver success stories — are there to articulate and describe not only their journey, but also the love, joy and freedom they have found in their lives today.

I'll let them speak for themselves. Their stories say it all.

I am so proud of them and so amazed by their courage and strength. They are women who are not just surviving, but thriving after abuse!

SOPHIA

Sophia wrote her Vision Statement shortly after meeting Susan in early 2004.

I am a woman of power who has made a positive impact on the world through my own healing, wellness and creativity.

I am a woman of power who has integrity and always believes in doing the right thing, even when it is challenging. It exposes my true character when no one sees me but God.

I am a woman of power who has embarked upon this earth to make a difference in other women's lives, to inspire them to achieve their highest level of humanity and cultivate the world with love.

Today I celebrate my life by being true to myself, being open to others and being filled with positive energy. This transformation has brought out the best in me, taught me self-love and, like a flower bud, allowed me to blossom into a beautiful rose.

Today I celebrate my life, which resembles the ever-changing four seasons — fall to winter, winter to spring and then spring to summer — secure that I can go forward with confidence and without fear of anything.

Sophia is a social worker who works with women and their children, helping them to make their families the best they can be. This work fulfills her life purpose.

VANESSA

When Susan first met Vanessa in early 2003, she wasn't singing. Today she is a singer again and in a healthy, happy marriage.

I was an abused woman for more than half my life. Growing up with an alcoholic parent, I learned early on to feel unworthy of love, self-respect or how to know the importance of having healthy self-esteem. When I began dating, I suffered many painful abusive relationships.

I left my last abusive relationship when we were separated by his arrest and the issuance of a restraining order. I sought help at a free counseling service and shelter for victims of domestic violence and sexual assault.

That's when I discovered a flyer promoting the My Avenging Angel Workshops™. Everything inside me said that I needed to check it out, and when I arrived one January morning I felt an instant connection to Susan. In the weeks that followed, she helped me find myself again, and I believe this was the start to finding my life's purpose.

You see, I have been a singer for most of my life. My abusive ex-partner was also a musician and we performed together professionally as an acoustic music duo. Linking the joy of singing to my own personal pain, I stopped singing for a time following the restraining order. Singing was something I had been doing since I was five years old. In my teens, I bartered work during the summers and school year so I could afford voice lessons at the studio down the street. I even received a lot of encouragement from strangers all my life and from those who heard me sing in the duo but for a time, what seemed like an eternity, I silenced it all because of the abuse.

In September of 2003, Susan held her first weekend retreat. The week prior to the retreat, I noticed an advertisement for a band looking for singers. I dreamed about singing in a band but why try? Susan encouraged me to sing some of my songs and play guitar for the women at the retreat. I received so much encouragement from Susan and all the women there, so the morning of the last day of the retreat, I ran back to my room, called the number in the ad, auditioned that week, and a few days later I got the call. I was the band's new lead singer! I've since sung lead with several bands and am busy recording demos for other songwriters.

The end of 2004, Susan was nominated for the Woman of Character award sponsored locally. Upon learning that she won the award, Susan immediately asked if I would write and present a song chronicling my journey to an abuse-free life. Here was yet another opportunity to showcase my talent — with an original song, not just a cover.

I wrote the song "Flying" after another of Susan's workshops in which one of the members described her skydiving experience. At that workshop, Susan put on some soothing background music and led each of us in reenacting the thrill of jumping out of a plane, falling through the sky and then pulling open our parachutes to float our way gently and safely to the ground. After that experience, I couldn't help but see the similarity between leaving an abusive relationship and the act of skydiving. Both require much mental and physical preparation, both take guts to "take the leap" (out of a plane in the case of skydiving), and in both we take our time searching for a safe place to land.

After performing "Flying" on the award night for the first time, the positive response I again received inspired me to write more songs about domestic violence. I created a publishing project to get these songs out to the world through the internet. Since 2006, my songs have been featured at community awareness events, marches, vigils and galas for Domestic Violence awareness worldwide.

Susan's work is like a life-coaching system of constant support and encouragement as we learn to put abuse behind us and live well as our best revenge. This is something that abusers never want for us.

While counseling helped me to find and stay on the right path, Susan's "seven-step" program was like a path of stones guiding me safely across an ever-flowing river. With guidance and encouragement, and a little soul searching, we can uncover our gifts to the world. I never imagined I would write songs to spread the word about domestic violence. Honestly, once I lost my voice to domestic violence, I thought I would give up music for good. Instead, I married another musician. He is a kind, loving and strong musician and activist who walks by my side. There is power by example, and there is reward for our suffering. Awareness, strength and second chances await.

VANESSA'S VISION STATEMENT

I am a creative, talented young woman seeking to reach out to other survivors of domestic violence through my singing and songwriting abilities, offering comfort and encouragement through the sound of my voice and the power of my words.

BETSY

Betsy met Susan in September of 2002.

Today she is remarried and in a healthy, happy relationship.

I was an abused woman for ten-plus years. I left the abuse on June 23, 2001, almost two years ago. I have been involved in several programs that helped me leave the abuse. Fortunately for myself and my two young children, we had a loving family member's home to seek shelter in as our first move. I later connected with the Women's Center in Plymouth, Massachusetts. Aside from just knowing they were there, I was beyond the need for their emergency-related services. A few months later I was tipped off by my daughter's school librarian about a woman (who I'll call Mary here) who worked with women in abusive relationships. I might add that this school librarian hosted my first calling when she guided me into one of her workrooms and asked me what was up because "my smile was not real and I was acting life." This was a few weeks before June 23, 2001. This acquaintance saw my pain. My work with Mary was like nothing else up to that point in my life. At our first meeting, I remember her words so well — that I had now recognized my placement in what was, for the loss of any other words, a "secret woman's club." Only women who have been so displaced, mistreated and led astray by abuse would be able to identify that in others. It is also from Mary that I found the book, Men Who Hate Women and the Women Who Love Them *by Susan Ford, which validated the sins of the man who abused me and shed some light on them for me. Mary, who worked for a nonprofit domestic violence organization in Massachusetts, told me to listen to my "gut," and that has proven to be a good guide. Moving to Connecticut brought me to Interval House, a domestic violence program in Hartford, where I met with a counselor and later joined the Tuesday night support group.*

It was there that I met Susan Omilian. She led a thought-provoking session one night and passed out flyers for her upcoming My Avenging Angels Workshops™. A few days passed before I dialed the registration line and placed my name on the attendance list for the September 2002 workshop. I really do not know why I wanted to go, other than my eternal search for some heightened awareness of real life and the reason why I was not living it. Knowing how I think about myself, my interaction would be all talk and little progression. The good part was that at least I was getting myself out and trying.

Ahh... the workshops... a lot of information. On the first day, Susan renamed my "gut" terminology with "the call." This is a term that describes an internal routing device within each of us if we allow ourselves recognition of its presence. Each of us in that workshop were there for whatever reason, but we got ourselves there. In one exercise, we wrote a letter to the Happy Person Inside Us which proved to be very interesting. I found that by the second sentence I welled up with emotion because I was writing to someone I had not connected with in a long time. It was a scary thought to be living so closely with that part of me and not know about it. We also talked of fears and negative energy and how they affect positive progression. It all seemed like the commonsense knowledge one would utilize daily in their actions, but when I saw where I was stuck, I could see how these negative patterns can influence our lives.

Breaking that cycle, sink or swim, after looking at it through Susan's perspective, meant making a choice between fears, limiting beliefs about myself and negative thoughts or more positive ones. Most of the exercises and information that Susan presented were refreshing and rekindled more thought processes for me to act on. At times it was hard. One place I struggled, and am continuing to struggle, was with setting short- and long-term goals. I can dream, and I really do want a lot. However, time seems to be moving so quickly. Between my children's needs and my inability to provide for them as I would like to, happiness only seems to circle around my head, waiting to come crashing down. Weeding through this rubble will happen in due time as I continue to learn about myself. It is not very often I tell that person inside me who I wrote to in my Angel Journal that I am happy, that she is with me and what a great job we are both doing, but I am writing. And without Susan's work, I would not be writing to that person at all. If I think back to the health of my inner self during the abuse, I am so saddened by the loss of myself during that time period.

My hope for other abused women needing guidance is that they are able to find someone as enthusiastic and positive as Susan. There is a great need for women to start believing in themselves. There should be no price for this kind of freedom.

A personal adventure with an Angel at my side!

SUSY

Susy wrote this piece when she first met Susan in September of 2002. Today she has a master's degree in Public Administration with a concentration in domestic violence studies and is in a healthy, happy relationship with a new partner.

I was an abused woman for seven years. I left the abuse about a year ago.

I have been involved in several programs that have helped me process my decision to leave and survive the transition, including a divorce support group at my church to help me with divorce issues, apart from the abuse. I also attended a weekly women's Bible study to share the word and live under the promise of God's strength as it relates to our personal lives. Interval House, the local domestic violence services program, was instrumental in supporting me through the crisis part of my transformation and was the place where I learned to identify my current situation and face my reality.

This was also where I found out about Susan Omilian. The counselor there saw the value Susan could bring to women who are recovering from the brokenness left after leaving an abusive relationship and encouraged me to attend one of Susan's My Avenging Angel Workshops™ in September 2002. If I had to pinpoint the single most valuable piece Susan provided for me, it would be the steps to wellness that she strategically guided us through. From what was a pit of ruins, she entered our lives with a hard hat and flashlight and helped us clear our way through the rubble, leading us back to safety. Anxiety, depression and worthlessness had left us all in the ruins, but from the safe zone she helped us get to we went on to set our short- and long-term goals. We now know that the steps between these short- and long-term goals are only steps, but we are in much better shape to take them thanks to Susan.

The hardest exercise that I can remember in Susan's workshop was writing a letter to the Happy Person Inside, which meant I had to realize I was disconnected from that part of me. Having to face whatever it was that allowed me to become disconnected was not easy. One of the lovely things about Susan's workshop is the bond created and shared by the women who have taken the workshop. Through these friendships of openness and honesty, which include Susan who opened her life to us during her teaching, we have gained much needed strength to be able to cope with our individual situations. This disclosure shared in a trusting, safe environment has been comforting in the face of uncertainty and knowing that whatever level we are at is acceptable — we are opening up the door to acquiring new levels of wisdom and healing.

What has happened to us is part of our journey. What we become is as good as what we are willing to reveal and work on. Resources are the key to facilitating these transformations, and programs like Interval House, which was a critical resource in the beginning for me, now exist where previously women have been on their own to figure out the rest of their lives. Susan's workshops have provided a place for the next critical step to be born — living well as the best revenge. The fact that her program is free of charge sends a far-reaching message that affluence has no weight in the development of our lives. My Avenging Angel is guiding me to my best revenge!

SUSY'S VISION STATEMENT

I am a woman of power who is strong, independent, driven to overcome social injustice and empower others through meaningful work, fortified by the spirit and in love with my family. Today, I celebrate my life by letting go of past hurts, rejoicing in independence, having dreams, loving my children, forgiving myself, embracing the future, cherishing my friends and family, acknowledging God, learning my truths and surrounding myself with angels.

DONNA

Donna wrote this piece below when she first met Susan in September of 2002 and she was leaving an abusive first marriage. Today Donna has a business degree, works as a manager for a medical billing company and is now in a healthy, happy second marriage.

I'm really not sure how long I was an abused woman. I met my husband when I was fifteen and married him at twenty. I'm forty-seven now, and we just passed our twenty-seventh wedding anniversary. We haven't lived together the past four months since he was arrested for hurting me. In dealing with his arrest, I became involved with Interval House, a domestic violence services program, which informed me of the My Avenging Angel Workshops™ to be held in September 2002.

To give you a better understanding of my life, I'll share with you some of my past. As I look back now, the abuse was there when we were dating. It surfaced in his verbal abuse, jealousy and control, which continued in our marriage. We were married six years before we had our children, and during that time the abuse didn't occur that much. My life was totally centered around him; we did everything together and very much wanted a family together. When the children came, and we had three in four years, my priorities changed and so did our income now that I was home with the children. As I became financially dependent on my husband, I always felt that gave him more power over me. Whenever there was an argument, it always came down to him name-calling and degrading me, even in front of our children. As the years went by and his drinking increased, the abuse happened more often and became more verbally violent. In fact, he has called me just about everything there is to call and accuse a woman of being. The abuse increased even more when I decided that I wanted to go back to school in 1998 to try to better myself so that I could go back to work full-time and seek better employment. As I continued to advance in my professional life, I became two different people — the one at work who was very confident and respected, and the one at home who was powerless and depressed. I always wondered if I would ever become one person. I can't begin to explain what attending the My Avenging Angel Workshops™ has meant to me. The major benefit it has given me is the support to survive and go on. It brought awareness into my life that I never had before. It gave me the strength to file for divorce. It helped save my life! Susan is showing me how to become the person that I most want to be and, most importantly, through the different exercises she has presented, she is visually showing me how to get there.

This workshop has totally changed my life! I'm not sure where I would be now if this wasn't made available without charge or any cost to me.

Dealing with the loss of my marriage and having to face the reality of my life is still a day-to-day struggle. I loved this man with all my heart, and the grief is sometimes so overwhelming, but from the knowledge and support that I have gained in participating in this wonderful program, I am beginning to rebuild my life and find the real me. I hope that this program can continue so that more abused women will have the opportunity to rebuild their lives and be given the hope to go on. Life is so wonderful with the start of spring and nature's new life. My life is starting over. I now have a feeling of being reborn, with happiness and thankfulness for the new beginning.

DONNA'S VISION STATEMENT

I am a woman of power who is moving forward and learning to take care of myself, guiding my children and showing them what the values of life should be. I am learning how to carry myself with self-respect, and I am helping others with what I have learned from my past experiences. I am showing them the benefits of having a peaceful life within your heart and then everything just seems to fall into place. In accepting our failures, we give ourselves the energy to move forward to a successful life.

POSTSCRIPT: DONNA'S HAPPY ENDING!

It's been six years since I wrote this piece, and I can guarantee you that your life will get better. In fact, my life has never been so wonderful. For any woman reading this book, you may doubt that you can change your life or that you can do this. Let me be living proof that not only can you do this, but also that your life will change and can be wonderful. It can be whatever you want it to be. You are the commander of your life, and by leaving an abusive relationship, you can take your life back and live it as it was meant to be. No one else has the right to be your commander except you. I'm not saying it will always be easy, but with great challenges come great rewards. Seek and reach out to people, including your family and friends, and most importantly, to organizations for domestic violence victims so that they can support and guide you. You can have your life back and be reborn into the life you were meant to live. If I can do it, anyone can! — Donna

RESOURCES

CRISIS INTERVENTION

For immediate crisis intervention services in your local community, contact:

- The National Domestic Violence Hotline 1-800-799-SAFE (7233) **www.thehotline.org**

- National Sexual Assault Hotline at 1-800-656-HOPE (4673) **www.rainn.org**

- National Center for Victims of Crime **www.victimsofcrime.org/help-for-crime-victims**

- Office for Victims of Crime, U.S. Department of Justice. **www.ovc.gov**

DATING VIOLENCE AND STALKING

- Break the Cycle: Empowering Youth To End Dating Violence **www.breakthecycle.org**

- Love Is Respect – National Teen Dating Abuse Help Line 1-866-331-9474 **www.loveisrespect.org**

- End Stalking in America **www.esia.net** provides information and assistance to potential victims and those currently being harassed, including a list of state laws against stalking.

- The Sanctuary for Victims of Stalking **www.stalkingvictims.com** offers sanctuary and resources on stalking to victims, how to identify stalking and deal with it through an online support group.

- Women's Law.org **www.womenslaw.org** is a project of the National Network to End Domestic Violence, providing legal information and support to victims of domestic violence, stalking and sexual assault.

DOMESTIC VIOLENCE

- National Network to End Domestic Violence (NNEDV) **www.nnedv.org** offers support to victims of domestic violence who are escaping abusive relationships and empowers survivors to build new lives.

- National Coalition Against Domestic Violence (NCADV) **www.ncadv.org** works closely with battered women's advocates around the country to identify the issues and develop a legislative agenda.

- Domesticshelters.org **www.domesticshelters.org** Free, online, searchable database of domestic violence shelter programs nationally.

- National Resource Center on Domestic Violence (NRCDV) **www.nrcdv.org** is a source of information for those wanting to educate themselves and help others on the many issues related to domestic violence.

SEXUAL ASSAULT

- RAINN — Rape Abuse & Incest National Network **www.rainn.org** operates the National Sexual Assault Hotline and has programs to prevent sexual assault, help victims and ensure they receive justice.

- National Sexual Violence Resource Center **www.nsvrc.org** provides leadership in preventing and responding to sexual violence through creating resources and promoting research.

- The Victim Rights Law Center **www.victimrights.org** is dedicated solely to serving the legal needs of sexual assault victims. It provides training, technical assistance and in some cases, free legal assistance in civil cases to sexual assault victims in certain parts of the country.

CHILD ABUSE

- Childhelp USA National Child Abuse **www.childhelp.org** directly serves abused and neglected children through the National Child Abuse Hotline, 1-800-4-A-CHILD®; and other programs.

POST TRAUMATIC STRESS

See information listed at National Institute of Mental Health website, **www.nimh.nih.gov**

BOOKS ON JOURNALING AND CREATIVE WRITING

One to One: Self-Understanding through Journal Writing and Life's Companion: Journal Writing as a Spiritual Quest by Christina Baldwin

The Artist's Way: A Spiritual Path to Higher Creativity by Julia Cameron

Journal to the Self: Twenty-Two Paths to Personal Growth by Kathleen Adams

Writing Down the Bones by Natalie Goldberg

Bird by Bird by Anne Lamont

BOOKS ON PERSONAL GROWTH AND SPIRITUAL DEVELOPMENT

Secrets about Life Every Woman Should Know: Ten Principles for Total Emotional and Spiritual Fulfillment by Barbara De Angelis

Anam Cara: A Book of Celtic Wisdom by John O'Donohue

The Seven Spiritual Laws of Success: A Practical Guide to the Fulfillment of Your Dreams by Deepak Chopra. Also, *The Path to Love* and *How to Know God*

Care of the Soul and *Soul Mates* by Thomas Moore

A Return to Love and *A Woman's Worth* by Marianne Williamson

Something More: Excavating Your Authentic Self and *Simple Abundance* by Sarah Ban Breathnach

You Can Heal Your Life by Louise L. Hay

Sacred Contracts: Awakening Your Divine Potential by Caroline Myss

Faith in the Valley: Lessons for Women Who Are on the Journey to Peace by Iyanla VanZant

The Gifts of Imperfection: Let Go of Who You Think You're Supposed to Be and Embrace Who You Are by Brene Brown. Also, view her TED Talks at **www.TED.com**

Mindfulness Meditation based on Buddhist tradition — See books by Jon Kabat-Zinn including *Wherever You Go, There You Are: Mindfulness Meditation in Everyday Life*

BOOKS & WEBSITES TO EDUCATE AND INSPIRE YOU

It Could Happen to Anyone: Why Battered Women Stay by Alyce LaViolette and Ola Barnett
www.alycelaviolette.com

Why Does He Do That? Inside the Minds of Angry and Controlling Men and *Daily Wisdom for Why Does He Do That?* by Lundy Bancroft **www.lundybancroft.com**

Macho Paradox: Why Some Men Hurt Women and How All Men Can Help by Jackson Katz
www.jacksonkatz.com

Trauma and Recovery: The Aftermath of Violence from Domestic Abuse to Political Terror by Judith Herman, MD

Beyond Trauma: A Healing Journey for Women by Stephanie S. Covington, PhD
www.stephaniecovington.com

I Closed My Eyes: Revelations of a Battered Woman by Michele Weldon
www.micheleweldon.com

Slow Hope: The Long Journey Home by Anita Swanson **www.anitaswanson.com**

The Verbally Abusive Relationship and Verbal Abuse Survivors Speak Out; On Relationship and Recovery by Patricia Evans **www.patriciaevans.com**

From Ex-Wife to Exceptional Life™: A Woman's Journey through Divorce by Donna Ferber
www.donnaferber.com

Miss America by Day: Lessons Learned from Ultimate Betrayals and Unconditional Love by Marilyn Van Debur **www.missamericabyday.com**

A Thousand Splendid Suns by Khaled Husseini, author of *The Kite Runner*

Coercive Control: How Men Entrap Women in Personal Life by Evan Stark

Scared Silent: A Memoir by Mildred Muhammad **www.mildredmuhammad.com**

Invisible Chains: Overcoming Coercive Control in Your Intimate Relationship by Lisa Aronson Fontes PhD **www.lisafontes.com**

MOVIES TO ACCOMPANY YOU ON YOUR JOURNEY

Sleeping with the Enemy (1991) with Julia Roberts — An abused woman gets a life!

Riding in Cars with Boys (2001) with Drew Barrymore — Based on a true story of a woman's life.

Billy Elliot (2000) — A young boy finds his dream in ballet despite his father's disapproval.

Erin Brockovich (2000) with Julia Roberts — A woman who doesn't give up and helps others!

Waiting to Exhale (1995) with Whitney Houston — Be happy with who you are.

Ever After (Cinderella) (1998) with Drew Barrymore — The best happy ending.

Thelma and Louise (1991) with Susan Sarandon — Girls rock even as they careen in a car over a cliff.

Fried Green Tomatoes (1991) — Based on Fanny Flagg's novel about the Whistle Stop Café.

Titanic (1997) — Rose lives on to find the life of her dreams.

Enough (2002) with Jennifer Lopez — An abused woman fights back.

What's Love Got to Do With It (1993) — The triumph of Tina Turner.

How Stella Got Her Groove Back (1998) — Stella takes inventory of her life.

Cry for Help: The Tracy Thurman Story (1989) — A true story about overcoming injustice and achieving social change.

The Burning Bed (1984), starring Farrah Fawcett — Still a riveting story.

The Color Purple (1995) with Oprah Winfrey — Based on Alice Walker's novel.

Muriel's Wedding (1995) with Toni Colette — The hapless Muriel finds herself!

Enchanted April (1991) — Rent a villa in Italy and see what happens.

A League of Their Own (1992) with Madonna and Rosie O'Donnell — A sports story for women!

Paying It Forward (2000) with Helen Hunt — No good deed goes unrewarded.

Shallow Hal (2001) with Gwyneth Paltrow and Jack Black — Beauty lies within.

Cinderella (2015) — A new version with Lily James of *Downton Abbey*. Best line, "I forgive you!"

Wild (2014) with Reese Wetherspoon — True story of Cheryl Strayed, who undertook a 100-mile solo hike as a way to recover from her mother's untimely death.

Eat, Pray, Love (2010) with Julia Roberts — A woman's quest to rediscover and reconnect with her true, inner self.

Saving Mr. Banks (2013) — The woman who created the Mary Poppins stories takes on Walt Disney.

Philomena (2013) with Judi Dench — Inspiring journey of unmarried mother to uncover truth about the son she was forced to give up decades earlier.

Frozen (2013) — A story of an epic journey to find Anna's sister Elsa, the Snow Queen, and put an end to her icy spell.

Enchanted (2007) with Amy Adams — The ultimate "real-life" fairy tale with a big production number in Central Park, New York City.

MUSIC TO SOOTHE YOU

Michael Hoppe: *The Yearning — Romances for Alto Flute* (with Tim Wheater), *The Unforgetting Heart, Solace* and *The Poet — Romance for Cello*

Raphael: *Music to Disappear Into I and II*

Movie Soundtracks: *Possession* and *Secret Garden*

Enya: including *A Day Without Rain* and *Paint the Sky with Stars*

David Lanz: including *Cristofori's Dream*

Loreena McKennitt: including *The Book of Secrets*

Thank you for reading the first book in Susan M. Omilian's Thriver Zone Series™ –

Entering the Thriver Zone
A Seven-Step Guide to Thriving After Abuse

Coming NEXT in the *Thriver Zone Series*!

Staying in the Thriver Zone
A Road Map to Finding Your Power and Purpose

Living in the Thriver Zone
A Celebration of Living Well as the Best Revenge

Connect with Susan about her books and her work with women....
www.ThriverZone.com

f www.facebook.com/ThriverZone

🐦 www.twitter.com/ThriverZone

📌 www.pinterest.com/susanomilian/thriver-zone

in www.linkedin.com/in/susanomilian

▶ www.youtube.com/susanom1

THRiVER
Z@NE™